Mutiny On The Western Front:

1918

Greg Raffin

16pt

Copyright Page from the Original Book

Copyright © Greg Raffin

First published 2018

Copyright remains the property of the authors and apart from any fair dealing for the purposes of private study, research, criticism or review, as permitted under the Copyright Act, no part may be reproduced by any process without written permission.

All inquiries should be made to the publishers.

Big Sky Publishing Pty Ltd
PO Box 303, Newport, NSW 2106, Australia
Phone: 1300 364 611
Fax: (61 2) 9918 2396
Email: info@bigskypublishing.com.au
Web: www.bigskypublishing.com.au

Cover design and typesetting: Think Productions
Printed in China by Hang Tai Printing

A catalogue record for this book is available from the National Library of Australia

For Cataloguing-in-Publication entry see National Library of Australia.

Creator: Greg Raffin
Title: Mutiny on the Western Front: 1918

TABLE OF CONTENTS

ACKNOWLEDGEMENTS	ii
FOREWORD	v
INTRODUCTION	ix
CHAPTER 1: 'THEY WENT WITH SONGS TO THE BATTLE...'	2
CHAPTER 2: THE REAL WAR AND THE PROPAGANDA WAR	15
CHAPTER 3: BIRTH OF A LEGEND	31
CHAPTER 4: MILITARY TRAINING AND DISCIPLINE	50
CHAPTER 5: DEALING WITH THE REALITIES	70
CHAPTER 6: MUTINY AND DESERTION	101
CHAPTER 7: THE MUTINY ON THE WESTERN FRONT	141
CHAPTER 8: ISOLATED AND LONELY BUT NOT ALONE	176
CHAPTER 9: NOR THE YEARS CONDEMN...	197
CHAPTER 10: WITH THE BENEFIT OF HINDSIGHT	229
CHAPTER 11: LIFE GOES ON...	255
APPENDIX 1: DEATH SENTENCES AND EXECUTIONS IN WORLD WAR I	270
APPENDIX 2: EXECUTIONS IN THE BRITISH ARMY, 1914–1918	272
APPENDIX 3: MUTINEER AND NON-MUTINEER OCCUPATIONS	274
APPENDIX 4: ALLIED FORMATIONS IN WORLD WAR I	276
APPENDIX 5: TERRITORIAL RECRUITMENT AND DIVISIONAL STRUCTURE FOR THE 1ST DIVISION OF THE AIF IN WORLD WAR I	277
APPENDIX 6: AUSTRALIAN 1ST DIVISION COMMANDERS DURING WORLD WAR I	278
APPENDIX 7: COMMAND STRUCTURE, 1ST BATTALION AIF AS AT 21ST SEPTEMBER 1918	280
APPENDIX 8: BATTLES IN WHICH THE AUSTRALIAN CORPS WAS INVOLVED IN FRANCE IN 1918	282

References	284
BIBLIOGRAPHY	309
ABOUT THE AUTHOR	319
BACK COVER MATERIAL	328
Index	331

This book is dedicated to those who felt a sense of shame or suffered anguish as a result of things they did, things they didn't do, or things that were done to them, during the Great War.

ACKNOWLEDGEMENTS

There is no doubt that the term 'mutiny' is an emotive one, and my decision to write about it was not made lightly. The decision to do so was very much a result of the fact that I was intrigued by the personal story of Rollo Taplin. I am extremely grateful to his grandson, Paul Cowan, for having made me aware of his story.

I was also impressed by Richard Dennison's award-winning documentary, *Mutiny on the Western Front*. It was a source of motivation and I was glad when Richard agreed to allow me to use the same title for this book.

Professor Peter Stanley (UNSW, Canberra) provided great support and encouragement during the process of preparing and amending my manuscript. He spent considerable time scrutinising my early efforts, and I gratefully acknowledge his assistance. His comments were fair, thoughtful and well-founded. Originally I was reluctant to name the mutineers, but he correctly pointed out that such information was now readily accessible and that to maintain their anonymity was to concur that they deserved to be shamed. I thank him most sincerely for the time that he willingly spent on my behalf.

Professor Stanley also suggested that I approach Big Sky Publishing. This led me to Denny Neave and his editorial staff. I have found them very helpful during the editing process and, as a result, what I thought would be a protracted process has been much easier.

As with my first book, I found that the community of those who read and write history tends to be very supportive. I made every endeavour to contact those writers and documentary makers whose works I drew upon, and on each occasion I made contact, approval was given. Special mention needs to be made of the research staff of both the Australian War Memorial (AWM) and the National Archives of Australia (NAA). On each occasion I approached them with a question, they did their very best to assist me.

Andrew Currey and Kelda McManus of the AWM were particularly helpful.

Once again, I found among my friends many who were prepared to listen to my endless anecdotes of interesting items I had uncovered during my research. Some of these people undertook to read parts of my manuscript and to suggest modifications. I would particularly like to thank Mrs Jenny Eather, Mr Allan Ridgewell, Mr Paul Cowan and Mr Ray Cooper.

I would also like to thank my immediate family for taking an interest in what I have tried to do.

Finally, I thank you, the reader. I hope you come to realise that this study grew from a desire to better understand, not from any desire to pry or denigrate.

Greg Raffin

FOREWORD

A century on from the largest and most destructive battles Australians have ever been a part of, we are told periodically (on the anniversaries of some of the major battles of the Great War) how well the troops of the Australian Imperial Force (AIF) performed. They took a leading role, suffered severely and, it is often claimed, achieved feats disproportionate to the AIF's size in terms of the overall effort of the British Empire armies on the Western Front. This may be true, at least in part, and Australians should never cease to be interested in their nation's part in the first of the great wars of the twentieth century, a conflict that had such a profound impact on Australia and its people that it remains the subject of dinner table, barbecue and coffee-break conversations a century later. However much Australians decry the Great War as futile, many cannot help being paradoxically proud of their forebears' part in it.

As Greg Raffin describes, on 21 September 1918 men of one battalion of the AIF declined to return to make an attack, the largest of the relatively few instances of 'combat refusal' in the AIF's history. Long a matter of embarrassment and shame for the AIF and the men involved, all of whom, as he reveals, suffered serious disciplinary charges, the 21 September 'mutiny' has been openly discussed for just on forty years. As he illustrates, it has been subject to a variety of analyses, looking at the military and social dynamics of one company of the 1st Battalion in the war's final months. He traces how the men's composition, military experience and leadership played out in the context of the exhausting demands of a unit that had seen practically continuous front-line service for weeks, if not months. He also examines how the AIF's unique combination of superb military skills and deplorable discipline created a force able to fight but unwilling to salute, and how its men's determinedly 'civilian' ethos led some to 'down tools' in battle.

Greg Raffin should be congratulated for directing our attention to the 21 September 1918 protest afresh, and for presenting it in an unprecedented light. Certainly, his analysis adds to what we know: he has approached the perplexing question of why these men did what they did from a novel angle. Greg's interest in this event stemmed from questions (which anyone interested in military history *must* ask) about how men in battle can possibly do what they do, and especially how they can act heroically. That interest, allied with the fortuitous discovery of the records of one of the 21 September 1918 'mutineers', led him to ask almost the opposite question: what moves men to refuse to return to battle? (I use the term 'almost', because these men were, as Greg shows, experienced and even decorated fighting soldiers: the opposite of heroism is not cowardice.) These men refused to continue to fight, an event surprisingly rare in the long, complex and tortured history of men in battle, and especially in Australia's short but crowded history.

Greg Raffin has found answers to his questions, ones that differ from those of the several historians, including myself, who have previously looked at this episode. He finds answers not so much in the workings of months of service, rates of wounding or promotion, as military historians do, but in the workings of men's hearts and minds in the course of a conflict like the Great War. In this, the story he tells, which will be new, and even surprising to most Australian readers, becomes not just a story about a group of exhausted, stressed and frightened Australian soldiers in 1918, but a story about humanity in war. His book is not only about what men do in war, but also about what war does to men.

I commend it to your attention as we approach the centenary of the events it describes.

Prof. Peter Stanley
UNSW Canberra

INTRODUCTION

It was an anonymous voice-over from a man I'd never met that piqued my interest in this little-known but poignant story from the closing period of the Great War.

In 1979, Mingara Films produced a First World War documentary called *Mutiny on the Western Front.* This was to become an awardwinning war documentary. For most of its duration, it discussed the horrors of trench warfare as experienced by soldiers on the battlefields of France and Belgium. Throughout the documentary, there were interviews with a small group of diggers who had experienced the daily decimation of those muddied and bloodied hellholes. They were prepared to discuss their experiences on the Western Front, but they did so with sadness and, at times, guarded comments. It was easy to see that for them, despite the passage of some sixty years, the torments and terrors remained.

These men were ready to talk about war in general, and their recollections were sobering. Over the years, I have read many personal accounts, listened to many interviews and watched many videos in which our diggers have recalled their war experiences. In none of these have I come across the view that they considered their time on the battlefield to be the best time of their life. Most were saddened or bewildered by their experiences; for many, the only positive aspect of their wartime experience was the mateship that evolved.

Not so for the anonymous digger expressing his views in this documentary!

His views were those of a very angry man, a resentful man whose resentment had not dissipated despite the passage of sixty years. He, too, had experienced those horrors. He, too, had fought long and bravely; he had achieved promotions and a bravery award recommendation. As a member of the 1st Battalion Australian Imperial Force (AIF), he had seen it all.

He, too, felt great sorrow at the waste of human life, at the futility of it all. He did, however, value the mateship and support of his comrades in arms. But this man, along with more than 100 of his comrades, had been court-martialled and gaoled for desertion as a result of a little-known mutiny that had occurred during the closing stages of the Great War.

Sometime later, I learned that a friend of mine was the grandson of this soldier. Neither he, nor any member of his family, including the digger's son and daughters, knew that he had been interviewed, nor that he had been gaoled for desertion, but they had seen the film and recognised his voice. They asked him if he was the anonymous digger. He admitted that he was, and also explained the reasons for his ongoing anger. Sadly, he passed away just two years later.

The truth was that these men were actually guilty of mutiny, an offence for which they could have faced a firing squad. Most of these men had been to hell and back. Some were newcomers, a minority may have been shirkers, but they were all treated the same; courtmartialled and gaoled. When the guns fell silent, these men were isolated and sent to a prison in England. They did not experience the euphoria which must have come with war's end.

A fog of mystery descended upon the families of many of the men involved. The men were not allowed to write letters, and any pay that had been allotted to be sent home stopped coming, hence the abiding anger of the anonymous digger.

I have been able to learn the life story (both before the war and post-war) of this particular man, and this story will be told here. Rollo Taplin's story, in itself, is an interesting one. However, it must be pointed out that this mutiny involved more than one hundred men, and that highlighting his personal story is in no way an indication that he was a ringleader in the mutiny that took place. My purpose has been to place in context the circumstances that led to this particular group of men taking such drastic action. As part of this process, the question of leadership will inevitably arise.

Some readers may feel that the men's anonymity should be maintained, but the simple fact is that today, their names and the details of their respective courts martial are readily accessible on relevant historical websites. Retaining their anonymity would also imply that they deserved to be shamed, without any effort having been made to better understand the circumstances in which they found themselves.

The episode that concluded Rollo Taplin's military service occurred just a few weeks before war's end, and has continued to be referred to as a mutiny; a 'refusal mutiny' wherein men walk out of the line rather than into battle. The very term 'mutiny' conjures up thoughts of disobedience, disloyalty and even cowardice. On discussing it with one friend, I was told, 'That matter is best left alone.' The implication was that it was taboo, and that no good could possibly come from reexamining it.

But history does not work that way.

My motivation for writing about this mutiny can perhaps be explained by a brief anecdote. Many years ago, another friend tried to convince me that in the second line of *The Ode,* the word 'condemn' should in fact be 'contemn'. I investigated this claim and found that he was wrong, but that the word 'contemn', in the sense of its meaning 'to view or treat with contempt' did actually fit the context. There is no intention to denigrate the memory of any of the men mentioned here, neither the mutineers themselves nor their commanding officers. I simply wanted to better understand their actions; to put myself in their shoes. My intention here is more like that of the instruction given by Oliver Cromwell to his portrait painter. The story of the Western Front needs to be told 'warts and all'.

Every story has more than one point of view. What could possibly lead men to take such an action? Were there any mitigating circumstances? What were the background circumstances? Has the full story been told?

***

There is little doubt that the Great War was a watershed in world history. The empires of four imperial powers (German, AustrianHungarian, Ottoman and Russian) were broken up, whilst that of Great Britain would never be the same again. The United States of America belatedly decided to become involved in European affairs, while Russia was beset by a civil war that preceded the emergence of a new and vastly different political system. Japan had brought to fruition its rapid program of industrialisation and had successfully enhanced its naval skills under the tutelage of Britain's Royal Navy (RN).

In addition, there were significant industrial and technological developments, some of which were to prove of considerable benefit in the post-war world. For example, considerable progress was made in the area of aviation. Other areas of transport and communication also witnessed technological advances. The world of medicine saw less spectacular advances, but they were there nonetheless. Of particular relevance to this story were the developments in dealing with mental health.

For the fledgling nation of Australia, the outbreak of the war was an extremely significant occasion. It was a mere 13 years since Australia had achieved the unification of separate colonies into a federation of states. Our national flag was even younger. Although we still saw Great Britain as the mother country, the potential was there for this new nation to begin using a separate voice, one with an Australian accent. The creation of the Royal Australian Navy (RAN) as a separate entity from the Royal Navy was seen by many as evidence of Australia's national emergence, even if Britain continued to make the important decisions concerning naval affairs. Thousands of onlookers lined the shores of Sydney Harbour to welcome the arrival of Australia's naval flotilla as it sailed through the heads on 4 October 1913. We were a nation. The depth of the independence that brought was yet to be measured.

When the British Empire entered the war in August 1914, the response from the new Australian nation was prompt, but even more notable for its expression of loyalty to the mother country. All sides of our political spectrum were united in the view that we should go to the aid of the British in their hour of need.

Andrew Fisher, the Prime Minister and leader of the Australian Labor Party (responding with what was probably the most notable 'one-liner' from the Federal government to that date) said, 'Australia will stand by our own to help and defend her [Britain] to our last man and our last shilling.' There were few, if any, public protestations of dismay over that comment. Given that in excess of 80% of the Australian population at that time had either been born in Great Britain or was descended from someone who had been born in Great Britain, this was hardly surprising. Public sentiment ranged from enthusiastic support to a view that we had a duty to offer assistance. Only a small minority were unmoved by any sense of imperial enthusiasm.

Well known is the fact that the government followed that statement with an undertaking that it would supply some 20,000 men to assist Britain. True to its promise, the recruitment of volunteers for the Australian Imperial Force (AIF) began immediately. Not so well known is the fact that it also began to recruit men to join the Australian Naval and Military Expeditionary Force (AN&MEF). These men were bound for German New Guinea and surrounding areas to wrest wireless communication bases that were essential to the German Pacific fleet from the hands of the Germans.

This particular military expedition has significant features in common with the mutiny upon which this story focuses. Both involved relatively small groups of Australian military personnel, and each of them occurred near the extremities of the time frame for the First World War; one occurred five weeks after the war began, while the other took place about eight weeks prior to its end. Relatively little has been written about either of them, and public awareness of either event is not widespread. My particular interests in the events of the Great

War tend to centre on the lesser-known incidents, those that deserve a higher profile or that demand a closer, less partial investigation.

Less than a week after war was declared, the British government 'suggested' to the Australian government that they might like to raise and equip a force to travel north and wrest the wireless station in German New Guinea and other similar wireless stations on the surrounding islands of the south-west Pacific from the Germans. The task was an important one because without these communication bases, the successful operation of the substantial German Pacific fleet would be seriously compromised.

If and when successful, the Australian government was to administer the captured territories, under British supervision, for the duration of the war. The British were quick to point out that any territory occupied as a result of this request would be considered British, and therefore the British authorities would decide the destiny of the occupied areas at the conclusion of the war. I refer to this campaign here partly because it illustrates the prevailing British view that Australia's role was to do their bidding.

For several decades, I had been aware of the success of this Australian military campaign, conducted well before Gallipoli. Six Australian military personnel died during the fighting that took place on 11 September 1914. Almost the entire fleet of the RAN had accompanied the AN&MEF. In addition, both the Japanese Navy and a New Zealand expeditionary force were involved in gaining control of wireless stations on the more remote islands. On 14 September 1914, the Australian submarine *AE1* disappeared, and the exact location of both the submarine and its crew of 35 men (16 from the RAN and 19 from the RN) has recently been discovered, over 100 years after it went missing. However, few secondary school history books even mention this campaign, and those that do dismiss it in a few lines.

My decision to research and write about this campaign came during the years just prior to the Centenary of Anzac commemorative events. The outcome was the publication in 2013 of a book titled *Australia's Real Baptism of Fire*. In launching my book on Remembrance Day 2013, Sir Peter Cosgrove, then NSW Chairman for the Centenary of Anzac, said, 'I could fire a cannon right now down George Street [Sydney] in peak hour, and I guarantee that I would not hit more than a handful of people who even know that Australia fought in New Guinea in World War I.'

My concern in writing that book had been to encourage greater recognition of the bravery of the men who died during that campaign. Similarly, few people know about the mutiny of 21 September 1918. With greater knowledge of this incident and the circumstances leading up to it would come a greater understanding of why the men reacted as they did. In short, both of these little-known events presented an opportunity to examine the reactions of men under fire.

My first book involved a group of men and a victory; this book involves a group of men and something vastly different.

Once I had begun to research the mutiny that occurred on the Western Front on 21 September 1918, I came to realise that not a lot had been written about this event. A large number of men, all of them members of the 1st Battalion AIF, had been court-martialled and sentenced to varying terms of penal servitude, but none of them had actually been found guilty of 'mutiny', instead being found guilty of 'desertion'. This particular battalion had taken part in the Gallipoli landings, and its members were later deployed to the Western Front, where they were involved in several significant battles.

My initial research raised a number of interesting questions. What actually happened, and was it a mutiny or not? Why did it happen to this battalion, and not some other battalion? Were there similar episodes involving other Australian battalions? If not, why not? Why did it occur when final victory was within grasp? Could it have been avoided?

There was also the question as to why so little had been spoken or written about it. It might be easy to assume that, being a mutiny, or at least an episode of shameful behaviour, no one wanted to discuss it. In addition, the nation as a whole had perhaps become more focused on getting on with its future rather than dwelling on its past. At the individual level, it soon became the norm for returning soldiers to avoid reliving the more horrific details of their war service and instead concentrate on returning to loved ones and the building of a happier future. This attitude of pushing the 'bad' into the past while moving towards the 'good' of the future is easy to understand, even after a century has passed.

However, surely such a strategy, whilst admirable, was unachievable for some of those concerned.

My investigations also quickly revealed that there were many other relevant aspects that needed to be examined, at least in passing, in order to discuss the topic more fully and in the proper context. These include the issues of heroism and resilience, bravery and cowardice, fatigue and shell-shock. Then there are other matters, such as military discipline and variations in the punishments for infringements, not just between various infringements and within each army, but also between the different armies of the various nations involved.

Anyone who has read about the Great War will be aware that as the war progressed, the public perception of its significance, and thus their reaction to it, underwent significant changes. This in turn impacted upon recruitment practices and enlistment figures, as well as the issue of conscription. Hence, matters such as government propaganda and censorship are also relevant here.

In short, I began to feel that I had opened the proverbial 'can of worms'.

However, I wanted to proceed. I wanted to form my own opinions and progressively draw my own conclusions about the circumstances which led to this 'mutiny'. I had to put the events of 21 September 1918 into their proper context.

I decided to pursue a chronological approach by briefly tracking the progress of the 1st Battalion and Rollo Taplin throughout the war in a series of stages; 1914–1915, 1916–1917 and, finally, 1918 and the year immediately following the war's end. Within each stage, the actual military events and changing attitudes towards the war, both at home and on the battlefield, form part of the discussion in order to provide an appropriate context for the events of September 1918.

The following narrative will attempt a brief chronological survey of the war's progress and the changing attitudes it engendered both at home in Australia and abroad on the battlefield. Both of these are crucial to a better understanding of why the mutiny occurred, as well as how it was perceived by outsiders. The actual event of the mutiny itself and its immediate aftermath, the field courts martial, will be fully outlined.

Rollo Taplin's early life was considerably different from what might be considered the norm. The military careers of certain of his comrades and the part they played in the mutiny will also be discussed. The story behind some of these men is quite enigmatic. This group included heroes and Gallipoli veterans, but it also included men who were ill-disciplined, and there was a significant number of men who had previously been wounded. They might all have been members of the 1st Battalion, but they were a varied group.

Finally I will briefly explore what history has had to say about this mutiny, presenting my findings in the form of an historiographical survey of opinions about the mutiny from observers who have discussed it at some length, either in isolation or as part of a broader study.

Aside from the field courts martial that were conducted at the time and a brief comment from Australia's official war historian Charles Bean, little was written about this incident for some six decades. The men involved were not willing to talk about the incident, and most chose to keep it to themselves. They lived with the consequences of their actions. Many felt a great sense of shame or anger, but they suffered these emotions in silence.

This is the story of Rollo Taplin and his shamed Anzac comrades.

Above all, it is a narrative; it is not a defence, or a justification, nor is it a condemnation. When discussing topics such as 'mutiny', complete neutrality is not really an option. It is an emotive term. A fuller understanding can only be achieved by examining relevant background details that were probably unknown by many of the men involved at the time, and are certainly unknown by most present-day observers.

This is a story about how people reacted to stress and how that reaction was determined not only by their character but also by the circumstances in which they found themselves. It is also a story of the contrasts and inequities thrown up by life. The response chosen by an individual to a particular situation will vary according to the time, the place and his or her character, as well as the particular circumstances in which they find themselves.

Within society, the heroic are often feted and lauded, while those who react less heroically or are perceived to be cowardly may be shamed and derided. With the hindsight of one hundred years, it is easy for the present-day reader to feel sympathy for not only those who were caught up in the horrors of the Western Front, but also the loved ones they left behind and to whom they later returned.

But can we also feel empathy? Can we put ourselves in their shoes and better understand what they were going through? If faced with the horrors of war, how would we have reacted? In a life-or-death situation, how would we have responded? Would we have reacted stoically, bravely or even heroically? Or would we have been found wanting?

XXV

Would we have taken part in a mutiny?

CHAPTER 1
'THEY WENT WITH SONGS TO THE BATTLE...'

(*For the Fallen*, **Laurence Binyon**)

CHAPTER 1

'THEY WENT WITH SONGS TO THE BATTLE...'

(*For the Fallen*, Laurence Binyon)

GRASSROOTS REACTION TO THE OUTBREAK OF WAR

After war was declared, it was soon realised that at some stage Australia was going to be involved. Some were quite enthusiastic in expressing their support for Great Britain, and even before the impact of government propaganda, there was obvious agreement that Australia needed to get involved. This support was evident in the print media, and also in diaries and letters written at that time. As history has proven, many expectations were unrealistic.

I think I ought to go, they will want all they can get ... and I think it is the greatest opportunity for a chap to make a man of himself ... (letter dated 18 May 1915).

...my motives for enlistment were more a sense of adventure and an opportunity to travel than patriotism ... many of us had a feeling of disappointment that the war would be over before we could get to France...

I may say that I was not influenced very much by patriotic feelings, but merely by the fact that my friends and relations were fighting, or were going to...[1]

Any reader of accounts of Australia's role in the First World War will have read comments similar to these. Those making such comments had no idea that there was a vast discrepancy between their aspirations and the reality, nor did they realise that, for many of them, the experiences they were to face would change them forever. An interesting story illustrating this enthusiasm to enlist involves a man who was also a journalist.

Conrad Constantine Eitel was a journalist who sometimes wrote articles for *The Sydney Morning Herald* under the nom de plume 'Darnoc' ('Conrad' spelt backwards). Although German by birth, he was one of the first men to enlist for the AN&MEF, and embarked on His Majesty's Australian Transport (HMAT) *Berrima* (a converted P&O vessel) on 19 August 1914, bound for German New Guinea. During this campaign, he was a member of the leading attack party, and as they moved down the road towards Bitapaka, circumstances arose that obliged him to act as an interpreter between the Australians and a German officer who had been taken prisoner, having been one of a group of three who were the first to arrive at the German wireless station.

So keen was Eitel to serve his adopted country that upon his return to Australia, he resolved to re-enlist in the AIF. Reasoning that he would be rejected, as it was now widely known that he was of German origin, he decided to re-enlist under his mother's maiden name (Easton). He was duly sent off to Liverpool training camp, but his true identity was soon discovered. The authorities decided to court-martial him, not for his German background, but because he had made a false declaration when stating on his enlistment papers that he had no previous military experience. Eitel was sentenced to some thirty days of imprisonment, but only spent a few days in gaol.

Eitel had previously played another role significant to the historical evolution of his adopted country. He had acted as secretary for Douglas Mawson's Antarctic expedition. This meant that he coordinated the fundraising within Australia in the lead-up to that expedition. Nor was he the only patriot from within the ranks of the *Australian Antarctic Expedition* of 1911–1914 who was later to enlist. A news article from December 1915 reported that 'the great majority of the members of the Mawson expedition are on active service.' The article went on to list some 13 members who had enlisted, including Edward Bage, who was killed in the Dardanelles.[2]

These men had just returned from risking their lives exploring an unknown region before once again setting off on a venture to an unknown destination that was going to put their lives at risk.

BAPTISM OF FIRE

The Australian-led campaign in German New Guinea and its surrounds was a military 'baptism of fire' for the new nation in the sense that it was the first time since federation in 1901 that the young Australian Commonwealth government had allocated and equipped Australian units heading for battle. The government also undertook the training of these men.

It was here in New Guinea that the reaction of Australian troops under fire was to be tested for the first time during the First World War. It was also during this campaign that the Australian government was to become enmeshed in an incident that came under public scrutiny back in Australia and had the potential to damage government recruitment campaigns. The reaction of raw recruits when under attack and government propaganda campaigns were both relevant, even if only in a peripheral sense as the war progressed.

It was a successful baptism of fire. The main wireless station (at Bitapaka, near Rabaul) was taken after hostilities that lasted for a day and cost the lives of six Australians. Within three months, all the other wireless bases in the area had been secured and the German squadron had left. This meant greater safety for the convoys that later ferried our troops to battlefronts like Gallipoli and those in Europe. About 1500 men had been deployed, and almost the entire RAN fleet had been involved.

An action took place on the road to Bitapaka that led to the first bravery award to an Australian during the Great War. Lieutenant Thomas Arthur Bond of the Royal Australian Naval Reserves (RANR) showed considerable pluck and initiative in an action that later earned him the Distinguished Service Order (DSO). Bond was born in Great Britain and had later migrated to Australia and joined the RANR. When war broke out, he was forty-nine years of age and working in Brisbane as an accountant. He was a man of considerable composure, not given to flights of fancy, and his opinions were valued by those around him. He was sometimes kindly referred to as 'grandad' by his comrades.

As the Australians advanced towards the German wireless station at Bitapaka, it was decided to split into two groups, each of which proceeded cautiously through the jungle on either side of the road. Bond found himself in charge of one of these groups, and he and his men came under fire as they proceeded. The men continued to move forward, and about a kilometre from the wireless station they came upon a group of eight Germans armed with pistols, along with twenty native New Guinean soldiers who were armed with rifles. To the surprise of the Australians, the Germans did not surrender. Instead, they began a discussion as to what they should do.

The situation was cleverly defused by Lieutenant Bond. Showing considerable bravery and great resourcefulness, he simply walked up to the Germans and relieved them of their pistols before they could react. The New Guinean soldiers were unable to do anything, as their officers were standing between them and the Australians. Captain Travers, who was there at the time, when later recounting the incident in an interview with war correspondent Frederick

Burnell, said, '"Splendid" is the only word I can imagine for his coolness.'[3]

Picture of five naval officers at Kangaroo Beach, Suvla Bay in August 1915. (L–R) Staff Surgeon Morris RANR, Lt Cmdr L.S. Bracegirdle, Lt T.A. Bond, DSO, [Australia's first bravery award recipient of World War I], Capt McRitchie RE, Major R.E. Jellicoe (Legion of Honour) [AWM P11155.007.001]

Bond had been under fire earlier that day, and his display of bravery and composure was not an isolated occurrence, as he was later mentioned in dispatches both at Gallipoli and in the Middle East. He was finally sent back to Australia after sustaining a gunshot wound to his upper arm. It is relevant to recount Bond's character and the circumstances of his bravery in terms of the discussion of the mutiny that occurred on the Western Front almost at war's end. The men involved in the 21 September 1918 mutiny were, for the most part, much younger than Bond. In addition, the sounds of battle and the extent of the fighting that was going on at that particular time were much louder and more widespread, respectively, than anything Bond had experienced. Lieutenant Bond was the only man to receive an award for bravery on that particular day, but 14 men were mentioned in dispatches.

While the circumstances would vary and the outcomes would differ, Australia and its citizens had set off on a new adventure, a journey that took much longer than originally anticipated. The men who took part in the German New Guinea campaign had signed on for a six-month deployment. Upon their return and discharge, some 71% of the members of the AN&MEF quickly re-enlisted in the AIF. This further illustrates the enthusiasm for the war effort that existed at the personal level at that time.

ROLLO TAPLIN: ONE MAN'S WAR

Rollo Taplin's family history suggests that he was destined for a role in the military at some stage in his life. His mother, Agnes Kate Marsh, was born in 1856 at Fort William in Calcutta.

Her father was a career soldier, having joined the army as a private at the age of 19. He worked his way up through the ranks and after 31 years of service, retired with the honorary rank of Captain. Serving with the 53rd Regiment, he had spent 16 years in India, as well as other stints in Canada, Bermuda and the West Indies. In 1869, while the family was still in Canada, Kate's mother died, and Kate was sent to England to finish her education at a boarding school.

Rollo Taplin's father, Thomas Taplin, came from a non-military, privileged background. He had been born in Worcester in 1859 into a family whose wealth was derived from breweries and railways. Thomas became an artist.

The 1884 wedding of Thomas Taplin and Agnes Kate Marsh was a society affair in Worcester, and they had five children while still living in Great Britain. However, because of Thomas's reluctance to do meaningful work, as well as his capacity to embarrass the family, his father banished him to Australia as a remittance man. As such, he became an emigrant who was supported or assisted by payments from his family. The family travelled on board the *Ormuz*, arriving in November 1896. The journey to Australia would not have been a pleasant one for Agnes. She had the task of looking after five energetic children while pregnant with their sixth child. That pregnancy was to culminate in the arrival of Rollo Charles Taplin six weeks after their arrival in Australia. Although of British heritage, he was Australian-born.

The family settled in Leichhardt, a suburb of Sydney, in New South Wales. However, the early days of the Taplin family in colonial NSW were to prove far from easy, as Thomas Taplin continued to be reluctant to fully confront his responsibilities. Sadly, after just 18 months in a strange land, his wife Agnes died from peritonitis. This left Thomas to care for a brood of six children.

Rollo was often forced to stay at home to look after the younger children, while his father, rather than dealing with the situation, tended to do his best to ignore it. Thomas was later to re-marry and sire a further six children, and it soon became apparent that the remittances sent from England were inadequate to support his now very large family.

Thomas Taplin decided to uproot the family of his second marriage and move to Melbourne, which dealt another cruel blow to Rollo. In 1908, when he was aged 12, he arrived home from school one day to find a note attached to the front door. The note instructed him to make his way to a nearby orphanage. His father had abandoned him. As will be shown later, this was not the only time in his life when Rollo Charles Taplin was to feel abandoned and let down.

Instead of going to the orphanage, he was taken in by an older sister who was now married. In return for her kindness, he was to work in her corner shop. At some stage over the next few years, according to his enlistment papers, he had some involvement with the 39th Militia. When war broke out, he was still living with his sister and working in the store, and he felt obliged to stay.

However, the call to arms, loudly amplified by government recruitment efforts and the tumultuous farewells of both the AN&MEF and the AIF, proved too great. On 11 July 1915, at the age of 18 years and 7 months, Rollo Taplin enlisted in the AIF. His enlistment papers show that he was 5 feet six and a half inches (about 168.9cm) in height and weighed 140 pounds (about 63.5kg). He was of dark complexion with brown eyes and black hair. His religion was given as Roman Catholic, and it was stated that he had some previous military service (with the 39th Militia).

The records show that Rollo Taplin was sent to the Liverpool training camp and originally allocated to the 2nd Battalion. However, either this was a clerical error or it was later altered, for he was eventually posted to the 11th Reinforcements for the 1st Battalion.[4]

CHAPTER 2
THE REAL WAR AND THE PROPAGANDA WAR

In war, truth is the first casualty
(Aeschylus, 525–456 BC)

CHAPTER 2

THE REAL WAR AND THE PROPAGANDA WAR

In war, truth is the first casualty
(Aeschylus, 525–456BC)

It soon became obvious that despite some optimistic predictions, the war was going to be more prolonged than many had believed. In November 1914, a large flotilla began the task of ferrying members of the AIF to the Middle East where, unbeknown to the men, they were to be brought up to readiness for the assault on Gallipoli. As Christmas came and went and 1914 faded into 1915, the AN&MEF's first deployment began to return from their successful campaign in German New Guinea. The recruitment campaigns were in full swing and enlistments, particularly in the AIF, were growing steadily.

An essential, and effective, part of this campaign was government propaganda. It is probably true to say that the nature of the government's attitude to and support for the war differed from that of the individual. To some extent, it was motivated by a desire to be seen as an independent nation capable of making a worthy contribution. Accordingly, it made promises to the 'mother country' such as that issued by Andrew Fisher. A change of prime minister had made little difference, as the government quickly made a promise to provide 20,000 men in Britain's hour of need. At the individual level, there was less patriotic fervour, but still strong support to right the wrongs done by Germany and its allies. In addition, there were those seeking adventure, those responding to encouragement from their peers and those who did not wish to be seen as shirkers or cowards.

Knowing something about why the men enlisted is helpful and relevant to an understanding of how they reacted when faced with the reality of modern warfare.

Both government and non-government propaganda (such as that later provided by the 'Coo-ee' enlistment drives) were significant in dealing with fluctuating enlistment levels. Also relevant was the change in public attitudes as the rising casualty rates became known and the realities and horrors of war hit home. The government made full use of newspapers and poster advertisements. Artists and photographers had a role to play, as extremely effective posters quickly appeared outside recruitment offices. Some years earlier, Kodak had begun to produce its 'concertina' cameras in large numbers, and with significant developments in photographic techniques, it was not long before it was possible to produce composite photographs in which two or even three pictures could be blended together into a single, more dramatic picture. The results were quite astounding. 'Threedimensional' pictures later appeared that showed much greater depth and detail. Such developments were to prove useful in the government's propaganda campaign.

The slogans that were used also proved to be quite effective. Advertising copywriting skills were developed and exploited by the government and Australians were invited to show their loyalty and get involved: 'Join the Sportsman's 1000', 'Won't you join me?' and 'God bless Daddy who is fighting the Hun and send him help'.

Private individuals also had a role to play. Well-known Melbourne businessman John Wren made a public promise that he would reward Australia's first Victoria Cross (VC) recipient with 500 pounds and a gold watch. He later honoured that promise by rewarding Albert (Bert) Jacka, whose bravery shortly after the landing at Gallipoli earned him the VC.

The circumstances surrounding Jacka's heroism were considerably different from those in which Lieutenant Bond had been placed. Jacka reacted while under enemy fire, while Bond had been under enemy fire earlier that day, but not at the time of the action that led to his DSO. Nor was the enemy fire that Bond faced as overwhelming as that at Gallipoli and, later, on the Western Front. In charging a Turkish trench, Jacka's actions were premeditated, while Bond's had been spontaneous but appropriate. The circumstances encountered by Rollo Taplin and his fellow soldiers in September 1918 were much more akin to those faced by Jacka than those faced by Bond.

Captain Albert Jacka, 14th Btn, VC, MC and Bar. Jacka was awarded the Victoria Cross soon after the Gallipoli landing. [AWM A02868A]

As time passed, word began to filter back of the opening battles in Europe, and so the nature of the propaganda began to change, as did the methods used by the government. The Minister of Defence authorised the production of films designed to attract volunteers and soapbox recruiters could be heard on street corners spruiking support for the war. The emphasis subtly shifted from the possibility of undergoing a paid overseas adventure or not letting down your mates to the grotesque atrocities supposedly being perpetrated by the enemy on innocent women and children.

Bill Gammage stated that 'as the length of the war manifested Germany's capacity, the Hun became a hideous monster, bereft of humanity, purveying an unearthly *Kultur*, shunned by the devil and damned by future generations of men.'[1] One poster shows a hideous enlarged image of a helmeted German soldier with a caption accusing him and his comrades of killing children and raping innocent women. Later in the war, a 1917 poster showed a group of German soldiers cornering an Australian alongside a rainwater tank. They had already killed his wife, whose body lay in the foreground. The caption read 'Will you fight now or wait for THIS?.'

Such government propaganda sought to boost recruitment numbers by alleging that the enemy was less than human based on their treatment of the civilian population of Belgium as they swept through that country in their attempt to encircle Paris. Meanwhile, the government was just as keen to portray the exploits of its own military forces in as positive a light as possible in order to sustain support for the war effort.

An isolated incident that occurred during the brief campaign in New Guinea provides an early illustration of the 'propaganda war' being waged between nations. It was quickly dealt with by the Commonwealth government, which was keen to minimise its potential impact on enlistment rates. It happened during the closing months of 1914 and was an embarrassing incident involving Australian activities. The incident was to generate an expression of displeasure by the British government.

A few weeks after Colonel William Holmes, leader of the first deployment of the AN&MEF, had successfully negotiated the terms of the German surrender, a group of disgruntled German plantation owners held a drinking session during which they aired their grievances. They felt that they had been betrayed by one Reverend William Cox, a British Methodist missionary. Taking matters into their own hands, they apprehended the hapless Cox and gave him a caning of some 30 to 40 strokes across his backside.

Holmes was incensed, and immediately ordered that the guilty parties be rounded up and brought in for punishment. This was quickly done, and Holmes, without conducting any sort of trial, decided to make the punishment fit the crime. He ordered that the local population and the Australian military forces gather in Proclamation Square in Rabaul to witness the Germans being similarly thrashed. However, one group was banned from attending. It was deemed inappropriate for New Guinea natives to witness one white man flogging another white man, regardless of the circumstances.[2]

Holmes issued instructions that no member of the militia was to take photographs of the punishment, but his order was in vain. Some soldiers concealed cameras under their uniforms and placed themselves in the second row of their formation. At the appropriate time, their comrades in the row in front of them would move to one side, allowing the cameramen to surreptitiously photograph the proceedings. They were not the only ones using their cameras. A German civilian took several snaps, and these ended up in a Brisbane newspaper office. An American fireman from a visiting steamer also took some pictures, which he later sold for a considerable sum to the German Consul at Surabaya. The Germans chose to use this incident as ammunition for 'return fire' against the propaganda campaign being waged by the British.[3]

In late December 1914, the incident was raised in the Australian federal parliament by Senator Edward Millen, the former defence minister. The next day Defence Minister Senator George Pearce investigated the matter and found that the inquiry had not been conducted in a courtroom.

In reality, the Australian government was more concerned about the fact that the incident had gained widespread international attention than they were about the legalities of the matter. The German government saw the propaganda value in using the floggings as a means of countering British propaganda, and used the incident as part of their efforts to gain the support of the United States, or at least its neutrality.[4]

The Australian government's inquiry concluded that Colonel Holmes's punishment was justified on the grounds that the caning of Reverend Cox had been a breach of martial law. Therefore, they took no action against Holmes. However, the government issued a clear directive that corporal punishment was not to be used again. Throughout this entire incident, the federal government had been reacting to opinions expressed by the British government.

This sorry affair aptly illustrates the manner in which wartime propaganda can influence public perception in just the same way that modern advertising can change consumer choices. It also illustrates how the British government was prepared to put pressure on the Australian government to respond in what it saw as an appropriate manner. This was later to become more obvious in relation to matters such as how deserters should be punished and whether or not the death penalty should be invoked as a deterrent.

While Holmes was dismayed that his return to Australia did not attract the hearty cheers that had signalled the departure of the AN&MEF, the other men were warmly welcomed by their friends and families as they trickled home over a period of several weeks.[5]

AUSTRALIAN REACTIONS TO AND READINESS FOR WAR

Just as 1914 witnessed Australia's introduction to the Great War, 1915 saw evidence of a growing commitment to the war effort within both the government and the community at large.

The federal government passed the *War Precautions Act*, which increased its power to pass and enforce any rules it deemed relevant to pursuing the war effort. There was extensive censorship of letters sent by private soldiers and newspaper articles written by journalists, and the federal government levied an income tax to help meet the cost of the war. Half wages were paid to women who joined the workforce, filling jobs vacated by men who had left to fight overseas. Thousands of German Australians were placed in internment camps (such as the one at South-West Rocks in NSW). Many Germans lost their jobs, and German schools and churches were closed. Some German place names were changed, for example, 'Germantown' became 'Holbrook'.

The powers assumed by the federal government under the *War Precautions Act* significantly increased its influence at all levels of society. Historian Bill Gammage reported that under the Act, there were some 81 offences for which offenders could be charged for expressing disloyalty, hostility or disaffection. He went on to outline the story of a Tumbarumba drunk who stated, in the Royal Hotel, that it was a capitalist's war and that they should not be fighting it. He was fined 100 pounds and only avoided a six-month gaol term because the authorities took into account the fact that his son was then fighting in the trenches at Gallipoli.[6]

There was considerable support for the war effort from within the wider community. Goods such as socks, bandages, chocolates and cigarettes were purchased with the proceeds of fund-raising drives and sent overseas for the benefit of Australian soldiers. These projects were run by bodies such as the Red Cross Fund and the Wounded Soldiers' Fund. Schoolchildren studied the progress of the war and helped to raise money for the war effort. The public also assisted with the issue of recruitment by organising and staging the 'snowball' recruitment marches such as the 'Coo-ee' march, which began in Gundagai in October 1915. Several other rural communities followed their example and initiated similar recruitment marches. However, these marches, while drawing the issue of recruitment to the public's attention, only resulted in a small number of enlistments.

The ubiquitous 'white feather' was another strategy that was employed.

The white feather had been the traditional symbol of cowardice used by the British army as far back as the 18th century. It supposedly harks back to the days of cockfighting and the fact that only inferior cross-bred cockerels show white feathers. In August 1914, Admiral Charles

Fitzgerald founded the Order of the White Feather, and women were encouraged to present a white feather to eligible men not wearing a uniform.

In time, this practice proved effective in persuading a number of men to enlist, and it spread to other nations throughout the Empire. However, it also presented problems when public servants, employed in what were seen as essential services, were presented with a white feather. Nor was the practice popular with serving men who were home on leave for medical or other reasons. Later in the war, there was an occasion when a British VC winner, who was on his way, dressed in civilian clothing, to a public reception in his honour, was presented with a white feather. As a result, the British instituted a Silver War Badge for service personnel honourably discharged because of wounds or illness. Later in the war, the Australian government introduced a 'rejected volunteer' badge.

However, in 1915, the focus of the Australian government continued to be the equipping, training and dispatch of men to the European theatre of war. This process had begun in November 1914 when a large convoy of troopships and its escorts had left Albany in Western Australia. The men of the 1st Battalion were part of that convoy, and Rollo Taplin was about to join their ranks.

ROLLO TAPLIN: RECRUITMENT, TRAINING AND OFF TO WAR

Why did Rollo Taplin enlist? It is not possible to accurately state the specific motivation behind Rollo Taplin's decision to enlist. He may well have been motivated by a patriotic sense of duty, or he may simply have been seeking adventure.

In view of his particular circumstances, it would be reasonable to speculate that he might also have been motivated by a desire to pursue a life of his own choosing. He could have decided to no longer be dependent on his sister for his accommodation and livelihood. Having been so cruelly rejected by his father, he may well have been seeking a 'sense of belonging', a feeling of being part of a group. For him and so many others, the army was capable of instantly providing a new set of friends. It was in the interests of both the individual and the group that they became a closely knit unit. Army training and discipline worked towards that goal.

After completing his training at the Liverpool camp, Rollo Taplin left Australia on 5 October 1915, bound for Egypt. On 6 January, he was taken on strength from 11th Reinforcements at Tel-el-Kebir, where there was a training camp for 1st Australian reinforcements. This camp was situated 110 kilometres north–north-east of Cairo and 75 kilometres south of Port Said, on the edge of the Egyptian desert. After completing this further training, he was then sent to join the British forces at Alexandria on 22 March 1916. There, he boarded the *Ivernia* on 30 September 1916, bound for Marseilles in France.[7]

CHAPTER 3
BIRTH OF A LEGEND

Every legend, moreover, contains its residium of truth, and the root function of language is to control the universe by describing it.
James Baldwin.

CHAPTER 3

BIRTH OF A LEGEND

Every legend, moreover, contains its residium of truth, and the root function of language is to control the universe by describing it. James Baldwin.

As the war progressed, there developed a clear distinction between the reports published by government sources and the reality as experienced by the front-line soldiers. With the passage of time since the Great War ended, certain aspects have been highlighted and, because of this particular focus, have achieved almost legendary status. For example, Australians have been keen to highlight the achievements of their own forces. Conversely, those incidents that did not reflect well on either the individual or the nation have been pushed into the background. A classic example of the former, for Australians, has been the Gallipoli campaign. Another example is the image of the Australian 'digger', based on the image of the men of the AIF as fearless and relentless when engaged in battle.

Relevant to this unfolding story is the public's reaction to acts of heroism. Australian heroes were acclaimed by the press, while those who did not live up to expected standards of behaviour, such as deserters and shirkers, were often, but not always, concerned about the reactions of those back home. Public perceptions of brave and heroic deeds differed greatly from those of less heroic deeds, which helps explain why so little is known and understood about the latter.

General public enthusiasm for the war effort continued well into 1915. Enlistment figures of 12,505 were achieved in June 1915, nearly double those for April that year. Total enlistments for 1915 were 165,912, but this fell to 124,352 in 1916 and then plummeted dramatically in 1917 to just 45,101.[1]

In reality, a terrible loss of life occurred during the landings on the Gallipoli peninsula on 25 April 1915 and later during the Australian attacks at Lone Pine from 6 to 9 August 1915. More than 2000 Australian casualties resulted from this particular battle, which has since become a significant part of Australia's heritage. After Bert Jacka displayed great heroism and was rewarded with the VC, the Australian government was quick to bring his deeds to the attention of the public. The first VC to be awarded to an Australian during World War I came on 19 May, 1915 just over three weeks after the landing at Gallipoli.

Much has been written about the horrors and bravery of Gallipoli, and it has become so entrenched in the Australian psyche that we tend to overlook the fact that many other nations and nationalities also fought there. They, too, lost their loved ones. Many Australians also, incorrectly, see Gallipoli as the 'blooding' of the new Australian nation. These perceptions partially relate to the nature and extent of the wartime propaganda. Australia is not the only nation to perpetuate perceptions that lack accuracy, nor were such inaccuracies confined to the First World War. This author is aware of an anecdote concerning a British postgraduate history student who was studying the Vietnam War some two decades after hostilities ceased and was stunned to learn that Australians had fought in that war, because up to that point in time, every book he had read on the war only discussed the involvement of the United States.

It was from the rocky shores of Gallipoli that Charles Bean, the official Australian war correspondent, began to pen his reports and records which, for him, in time, would clearly distinguish the Australian soldier from his British counterpart. The outcome is sometimes referred to as the 'Digger myth', and often revered as the 'Anzac legend'.

The mutiny that occurred on 21 September 1918 has, for some observers, been seen as a betrayal of the 'Digger myth'. For some, the mutiny seriously questions the 'Anzac legend' perception of the Australian soldier. It is relevant, therefore, to briefly examine the tenets of this myth or legend. It is equally relevant to ascertain in which particular battles the 1st Battalion was involved, as those battles constituted part of the background circumstances leading up to the mutiny.

THE DIGGER MYTH

Central to the Digger myth is the concept of egalitarianism. Jack was seen to be 'as good as his master'. To many members of the AIF, an officer gained respect not merely because of his rank, but also as a result of how he related to those below him. Respect had to be earned. It has been said that Australian soldiers did not regard themselves as saluting officers in uniform; they preferred to salute the man, not the uniform. Another key factor is the ability of the individual soldier to use his own initiative. In volume VI of his official history of the war, Charles Bean described it in these terms:

'Yet at heart even the oldest Australian soldier was incorrigibly civilian ... he never became reconciled to continuous obedience to rules ... His individualism had been so strongly implanted as to stand out after years of subordination...

'His outlook contrasted sharply with that of most English soldiers of the time, whose discipline was largely founded on the social division of their nation into upper, middle and lower classes...

'He was the easiest man in the world to interest and lead, but was intolerant of incompetent or uninteresting leaders.'[2]

This last point, regarding leadership, is crucial to fully understanding the circumstances surrounding the mutiny involving Rollo Taplin and his comrades. It was also central to his lifelong anger stemming from the outcome of that mutiny.

Most historians seem to believe that the qualities of egalitarianism, resourcefulness, mateship and distrust of authority, all elements of the Anzac legend, emerged from the horrors of Gallipoli. If one man fostered this image more than any other person, then that man was Charles Bean. These same qualities were discussed by Russel Ward in his 1958 book *The Australian Legend*. Ward believed that they evolved from the experiences of rural workers in the Australian bush. Thus, the Anzacs have sometimes been seen as the sons of these bushmen.

The colourful stories of the British journalist Ellis AshmeadBartlett helped create the legend of the fearless Anzac. Even Britain's poet laureate, John Masefield, added to it by referring to the Anzacs as the finest body of men brought together in modern times. Bean may not have been the first to delineate the key elements of the Anzac legend, but he best outlined it, enshrined it and made it part of our history.[3] It is not my purpose here to identify the origins of the Anzac legend. However, discussion of its main tenets is relevant to the central focus of examining the motivation of the men involved in the events of 21 September 1918.

The Anzac legend stated, or at least implied, that the Australian soldier was a better and more effective soldier under battle conditions than many of his counterparts from other countries. An anecdote that underlines this belief comes from the war diary of Sydney Young. On 15 September 1918, he wrote that:

'A Yankee who could speak German asked a prisoner if he thought they were winning the war. He said, "Yes. God is with us.".' The Yankee said, "That's nothing, the Australians are with us."'[4]

In 2008, Dale Blair, in his book *Dinkum Diggers: An Australian Battalion at War*, used the wartime experiences of the 1st Battalion AIF to analyse the Anzac legend. He examined the contribution of this battalion at different stages of the war, from the landing at Gallipoli in 1915 to battles such as Pozieres in 1916, Bullecourt in 1917 and the attacks on the Hindenburg line in 1918. This study attracted considerable discussion at the time of its publication. Blair concluded that:

'With the exception of 1918, it could not be said that the experiences of the 1st Battalion in the conduct of battles, raids and patrols illustrated the abilities defined by the "digger" stereotype. Too many mishaps occurred to support an argument that advances natural-born abilities.'

Blair went on to argue his belief that the actions of the 1st Battalion in pursuit of victory during 1918 did, however, provide 'a compelling conclusion ... The magnitude of the successes achieved, and their interpretation, has advanced the standing of the Australian soldier.' Moreover, these successes were achieved more as a result of improved training techniques and planning, as well as 'an aggressive doctrine of the AIF'.[5]

Blair's study did not deny the excellent fighting qualities of the Australian digger. He rightly pointed out that it was most evident on those occasions when experienced troops, such as those of the British Army, were nearby and in a supportive role. He also questioned whether or not these fighting qualities were in existence throughout the entire war, and whether they were innate or the result, at least in part, of military training procedures. His was an important point of view, but it was questioned on the basis of his using only a limited sample, namely, the 1st Battalion. It was also unpopular with many who strove to perpetuate the Anzac legend.

Bean had implied that a majority of the men of the 1st Battalion were from the Australian bush, and Blair correctly pointed out that this was not the case. A majority of the initial enlistments were from Sydney, as was Rollo Taplin. More relevant here is the fact that it was from within the 1st Battalion AIF that the mutiny of 21 September 1918 occurred, and it was to this battalion that Rollo Taplin was posted.

1st BATTALION AIF WAR SERVICE

The 1st AIF Battalion had been formed shortly after war was declared in August 1914. Within two months, men of the 1st Battalion were embarked and after assembling with other troop transports at Albany in Western Australia, set off for Egypt, arriving there on 2 December 1914. They landed at Gallipoli on 25 April 1915, as part of the second and third waves. The battalion fought at Gallipoli for the entire campaign. During the battle of Lone Pine, two of its members, Captain Alfred Shout and Lieutenant Leonard Keysor, were awarded the VC for their valour. Captain Shout's heroism was sustained over a period of several hours and, like all instances of such valour, was an inspiration to many of those around him. Unfortunately his bravery cost him his life, and so his VC was a posthumous award.[6]

Among those who served during the Gallipoli campaign were 11 Australian soldiers who were destined to be part of the group caught up in the events of 21 September 1918. These men were from diverse backgrounds, and served at Gallipoli for varying periods. Three of them took part in the initial landings, while others arrived near the end of the campaign and were there for little more than a month. It is not possible, based on their service records, to determine which of them knew each other, let alone learn who among them became close friends. These records are for administrative purposes, and usually only record enlistment details such as place of birth, age at time of enlistment and place of enlistment. Beyond that, the most common details to be found include hospital admissions, wounds if any, disciplinary infringements and commendations for bravery.

The three men from this group who were there at Gallipoli from the beginning form an interesting trio. Two of them, Private Arthur Lawrence, a blacksmith striker who had been born in Quirindi in NSW and Private William Case, who had enlisted at Rosehill in NSW, were 31 and 28 years old, respectively, at the time of their enlistment, and were possibly somewhat older than most of their comrades. The third man, Private Ernest Stokes, a bushman from Condobolin in NSW, was only 21 when he enlisted. However, as the war progressed, it became apparent that behaviour, not age, was the common denominator among the three men. Privates Stokes and Case were to prove more than a handful for their officers, as both of them had significant difficulties in coming to terms with army discipline. Both men became repeat offenders, and the consequences for them were severe.

Many observers would condemn men such as Privates Stokes and Case for their poor disciplinary records, particularly as they were members of a military force. However, there is a need to consider the circumstances in which each man now found himself. The behaviour of a man under normal conditions can often be vastly different to that of the same man under conditions that threaten his continued existence. Similarly, there is a need to better understand the circumstances that lead to men taking actions that would ordinarily be viewed as rebellious, even mutinous.

The military authorities were soon to learn that such ill-disciplined behaviour did not necessarily mean that the men were incapable of heroic behaviour. There were men who were both larrikins and heroes, men who were occasionally punished for poor discipline but who later showed great courage under fire. Merely surviving for that lengthy period of time was an achievement in itself.

By the time of the 1918 mutiny, three of this group of 11 men had been promoted to the rank of Corporal or Lance Corporal. One of these men was Private, later Lance Corporal Richard Beggs, a 25-year-old labourer from Liverpool in NSW. Beggs did not arrive at Gallipoli until near the end of the campaign. Private Ernest Besley, who was two years older than Rollo Taplin at the time of his enlistment and who had enlisted just one month earlier than Taplin, was shipped to Gallipoli from Alexandria in mid-October 1915. However, fate was later to draw them together when they both arrived in France on board the same transport ship.

Their experiences on the Western Front were to prove remarkably similar, including their promotions to the rank of non-commissioned officers (NCOs). A similar example was that of Joseph Brissett. He had been one of the first to enlist, on 17 August 1914, and at that time had been just 20 years old. He, too, was later transported to the Western Front on board the *Ivernia*, along with Besley and Taplin, and was to experience similar events as them, but with a different outcome.

Conversely, Private William Robson, a 19-year-old motor engineer and draughtsman from Liverpool in NSW, who was almost the same age as Rollo Taplin and who had enlisted on almost the same day, embarked for Egypt about a month after Taplin. Fate and chance were to play a big part in the lives of the men of the AIF.

The service records of this particular group of men include few obvious indicators that they contributed to the part of the Anzac legend associated with heroism and valour, nor is there any indication that they failed to 'step up' and carry out their battle orders in the manner expected of them. For the most part, they completed their duties to the best of their abilities. Joseph Brissett, who was born in Murwillumbah in far northern NSW but enlisted at Randwick in Sydney, showed considerable pluck. He was promoted to the rank of corporal in May 1915, and at about the same time sustained a gunshot wound to his left shoulder.[7]

Because of the horrific conditions that prevailed at Gallipoli, some of the diary entries of the men began to indicate a growing sense of despair, even rebelliousness. Even at this early stage in the war, some men privately harboured mutinous thoughts. Private John Gammage became angry at the way they were treated by some of their officers, and said he 'would not care if 75 per cent of our officers had a wooden cross over his head.' He went on to say that 'if [I am] ever asked to dig a dugout for one or wash their shirts I will be shot at daybreak for refusing to obey an order on Active Service.'[8]

Given that the men who were sent to Gallipoli were among the first to be subjected to the horror that was trench warfare, it can hardly be seen as surprising that some would react in this way. The behaviour of others seemed to alternate between a struggle to survive and episodes of obvious disobedience. One such man was Private Arthur Mullins, a labourer from Liverpool in NSW who was barely 23 years old when he enlisted on 13 April 1915. Within three months he had left Australia, and later joined the 1st Battalion at Gallipoli on 6 August 1915.

He managed to survive the Gallipoli campaign, but just a few weeks after his return to Alexandria he was found guilty of being absent without leave (AWL). Two months later, in March 1916, he was charged with breaking camp while under arrest. Mullins travelled to Marseilles on board the *Ivernia* at the same time as Rollo Taplin, but within seven months he had been charged with committing a further three offences. Two of these related to being AWL, while the other was a charge of drunkenness.

Yet Mullins was not totally unaware of the role he was expected to play, and was twice wounded in action. In November 1916, he sustained a gunshot wound to his left side that resulted in his spending some time in a British hospital. He was wounded in action again the following year, this time a gunshot wound to his left shoulder, which resulted in more hospital treatment in Britain. During that same year, he committed a further three disciplinary indiscretions. It would seem that, possibly as the result of his situation, Private Mullins had developed an element of recklessness.[9]

Historians such as Peter Stanley have noted that, in general terms, the 'profile' of those Australians who enlisted in 1914 and 1915 differed from that of men who enlisted in 1916 and later years. This was particularly true in relation to their age and marital status. The 1914 and 1915 men later came to deride those who enlisted in 1916 and the following years as 'deep thinkers' and 'cold footers'.[10] Slightly less than 25% of the men who were later to be charged with mutiny had enlisted before 1916. Also interesting is the fact that despite Dale Blair's finding that the majority of the men in the 1st Battalion were from Sydney, 42% of this group had been born in rural NSW, with only 26% born in Sydney. However, it is feasible that many of those who were born in country areas later moved to the city in search of work, and therefore enlisted in Sydney.

Despite the valour and determination of the allied forces, little progress was made, and the casualty rates grew. Initially, this had little or no impact on enlistment rates, and there are a number of reasons for this. It took some time for news from the front to filter back home, but more relevant was the fact that all communications, whether private or from the media, were heavily censored. All letters from the front were carefully vetted and news reports filed by journalists at Gallipoli were read by the military hierarchy before being dispatched. Charles Bean was often frustrated by the degree to which his reports were censored and the facts distorted.

Ultimately, it became impossible to hide the reality of war from the Australian public. Far too many families were receiving the dreaded knock on the door, followed by a visit from the local clergyman. Soon, many back home could say that they knew 'so-and-so' had been killed, while at the same time hoping that similar news regarding their own loved ones would not come their way.

The situation for the soldiers on the battlefront was vastly different. The impact of the deaths and injuries occurring around them was horrifying and immediate. They could not hope that Death would not call, for they knew that it had called already. It is difficult for the non-participant, both at that time and decades later, to imagine the impact that such a situation was having on those who were forced to endure it. Those who had enlisted enthusiastically, hoping to take part in a 'turkey shoot', were now seeing circumstances that were vastly different from their prior expectations.

However, the men at the battlefront could not ignore their plight; they could only try to deal with it. How they dealt with it has become the focus of much discussion.

From Gallipoli, the battalion returned to Egypt before sailing for France as part of the transfer of four Australian divisions to the Western Front in March 1916. Four of the

Gallipoli veterans were to travel to Marseilles on board the transport ship *Ivernia,* the vessel that had brought Rollo Taplin to the Western Front. These five men were later to be linked together again in entirely different circumstances. What they would come to learn was that initial expectations and harsh realities could be vastly different.

Back in Australia, strategies were needed at the government level to maintain enlistment levels so that the undertaking given to both the British government and the men at the battlefront could be honoured. This would involve recruitment drives, as well as a minimisation of the efforts of any who strove to undermine or even criticise the war effort. Morale needed to be boosted, both on the home front and in the trenches. Both the government's propaganda encouraging a greater commitment to the war effort and censorship of anti-war opinions continued to play a key role in eliciting further enlistments.

For the Australian military authorities, the challenge was to maintain morale amongst the men in uniform and to encourage courage and resilience, while discouraging apathy, indifference and shirking, as well as any form of what could be called cowardice. This task took on a greater dimension for Australia more so than for many other countries, whose armies also comprised volunteers, and thus the sanctions for offences such as desertion and mutiny also differed from those of other countries. Their strategies were focused on the military training provided to the raw recruits because they needed to bolster the men's courage, resilience and discipline, as well as establishing a sense of cohesion within the group.

From the perspective of the soldier in the front-line trenches, it had already become apparent that there was a need for each and every one of them to deal with the realities they were now facing. In broad terms, they could either confront the situation or they could choose to remove themselves from it. In achieving the former objective, most men developed and employed particular 'coping mechanisms'. However, not every man was able to deal with the situation facing them. Some men suffered medical traumas, both physical and psychological, while others shirked their responsibilities and even ran away. It was this latter group of men who, later, were to be misunderstood or, even worse, derided and shamed.

CHAPTER 4
MILITARY TRAINING AND DISCIPLINE

Courage is will-power, whereof no man has an unlimited stock; and when in war it is used up he is finished. A man's courage is his capital and he is always spending. The call on the bank may only be the daily drain of the front line or it may be a sudden draft which threatens to close the account.
**Lord Moran (Charles McMoran Wilson),
WWI British Army doctor**

CHAPTER 4

MILITARY TRAINING AND DISCIPLINE

Courage is will-power, whereof no man has an unlimited stock; and when in war it is used up he is finished. A man's courage is his capital and he is always spending. The call on the bank may only be the daily drain of the front line or it may be a sudden draft which threatens to close the account.
Lord Moran (Charles McMoran Wilson), WWI British Army doctor

By the end of 1915, it was readily apparent that the nature of the fighting that was taking place on the other side of the globe was, for some, vastly different to their expectations. The war was not going to end quickly, nor was it the mobile warfare for which they had been trained. Both sides were bogged down in a stalemate. It was therefore very likely that this situation would affect enlistment rates back home, and also the morale of the troops at the battlefront.

Before 1914, the Australian government had created both a citizen militia and a navy, but it relied heavily on the British services' leadership in the area of military training. For example, competent officers from the RN were seconded to the RAN, and the same general approach was later used in training men for the AIF. Training was sometimes, but not always, conducted by British military or naval officers, and when Australian personnel took charge, they tended to follow the lead of their more experienced allies.

It is not the intention here to examine and discuss those training techniques. However, it is of benefit to briefly examine their potential effectiveness in bolstering the courage, resilience, loyalty and discipline of the men who underwent that training. What better way to do so than to examine the views of a knowledgeable man who not only went through that system of training, but also undertook a dedicated study of the qualities that were essential to good military practice and basic to heroic behaviour? In addition, this officer also provided extensive commentary on the factors that tend to erode courage and discipline, as well as those that contribute to breakdowns, both personal and in group morale. A brief examination of his conclusions will facilitate a greater understanding of why breakdowns in military discipline, leading to desertion and mutiny, sometimes occurred.

This man, Lord Moran, was a witness to the horrors of the Western Front, and was also involved in the events of the Second World War. In addition, reference is made to the views of another military officer, Sir Peter Cosgrove, who fought in the Vietnam War and whose views, in many ways, echo those of Lord Moran.

Lord Moran, who is quoted at the start of this chapter, was well qualified to discuss the issue of why some men ran from danger or failed to deal with it and broke down, whilst others reacted heroically, sometimes culminating in a bravery award being presented as an acknowledgement.

THE SUBSTANCE OF COURAGE

Charles McMoran Wilson (1882–1977), later Lord Moran, served on the Western Front during the Great War as a doctor in the Royal Army Medical Corps (RAMC). During this time, he kept a diary and made a particular study of the impact of the horrors of war on the men around him. However, he was not just an analytical bystander; he was himself awarded for his bravery and contribution to Britain's war effort. He was awarded the Military Cross in 1916 for services during the Battle of the Somme, and was also awarded the Italian Silver Medal of Military Valour in 1917, in addition to twice being mentioned in dispatches.

After the war, Charles McMoran Wilson had a distinguished career. He was Dean of St Mary's Hospital Medical School from 1920 to 1945, a prominent scientist, and President of the Royal College of Physicians from 1941 to 1950. He was knighted in 1938 and made a Baron in 1943. During the Second World War, he was again closely associated with the war effort by virtue of being Winston Churchill's personal physician.

In 1945, he published his book *The Anatomy of Courage*, which drew heavily on his Great War recollections, as well as his knowledge of World War II. This book has been widely quoted by those who have endeavoured to investigate and analyse the issues of heroism and cowardice. In many ways, it emulates the age-old discussion relative to phenomena such as intelligence and personality. Which is the more influential factor in the development of a person's character? Is it the individual's heredity, or his environment; is it his innate character, or the military training he experienced?

In this short but absorbing book, Lord Moran considered that the keystone to courage was what he called 'Character'. When using this term, he was referring to a man's 'substance', his 'core', his 'spine' or, alternatively, his lack of these qualities. Without dwelling on whether a man's character came about as a result of genetic or environmental factors, he concluded that 'A man of character in peace is a man of courage in war', and 'Man's fate in battle is worked out before the war begins.' However, he also believed that military training could bolster each man's character.

His observations led him to conclude that there were factors that could arise during the course of a war that led brave men to be less heroic, but that 'these men apart, the last war (First World War) signally failed to turn men of sound stock into cowards.'[1] This opinion is highly relevant to any discussion about the motivating factors behind the mutiny of 21 September 1918. The stoicism, resilience and bravery of these men, as well as any cowardice or ill-discipline on their part, are all relevant to forming a balanced opinion of their behaviour. Each man has a certain level of resilience to draw on before he reaches the point where he can no longer go on.

In more recent times, another observer who has studied issues such as bravery and resilience is Sir Peter Cosgrove. He, too, was awarded the Military Cross in 1969 for his actions during the Vietnam War. After seeking his views on bravery and resilience, his reply gave the impression that, at some point in his training and subsequent distinguished military career, he had been made aware of the views of Lord Moran (or at least someone who endorsed those views).

On the broad topic of courage, Sir Peter alluded to Lord Moran's analogy of courage being like a bank account from which the individual can make withdrawals when he stated:

'One [closing] remark is on the notion of a "bravery bank"; it's a useful if prosaic way of describing the limitations on any human's capacity for risk-taking. Equally though, I could mount an argument that "deposits" might be made to such a bank by rest and respite, by intensive training and indoctrination (effectively in reducing risk) and by mental health professional alleviation of accumulated stress.'[2]

Lord Moran was not dismissing the role of environmental factors relevant to heroic behaviour. For the men at the battlefront, the most crucial of these factors came through the vehicle of military training. He identified four key factors as critical to the management of fear. These were 'Selection', 'Discipline', 'The Support of Numbers' and 'Leadership'. It is not the intent here to deal in detail with his reasoning on these conclusions, but some observations are worthy of special mention.

In discussing 'Discipline', he had this to say about the Australian soldiers:

'The Australians of the last war (WWI) were magnificent fighting stock, but for discipline in the sense in which we use that term they cared nothing ... An independent spirit was native to them; they were on good terms with themselves ... they could not believe that discipline as we understand that term was necessary. They got on quite well in battle without it.'[3]

In discussing 'The Support of Numbers', Lord Moran was essentially referring to teamwork and a sense of cohesion. He felt that in working towards better discipline and morale building, a sense of being part of a team was critical. This is a very important concept for a military unit, and it is also an interesting one. When viewing documentary interviews or listening to recorded interviews with men who had previously fought in the First World War, it is quite noticeable that they repeatedly refer to 'mateship', to 'looking out for your mates'. This is basically what 'The Support of Numbers' means.

When discussing how a particular body of men react as a group in a particular situation, a discussion of 'The Support of Numbers', of 'mateship', is essential. This is even more relevant when the situation is stressful. This aspect will come under close scrutiny later in a discussion of how and why the men of the 1st Battalion reacted as they did on 21 September 1918.

In discussing 'Leadership', he felt that a good leader didn't just lead men, but also contributed towards the establishment of a cohesive atmosphere.[4] This was best achieved by getting to know them better, both their strengths and their weaknesses. In short, a good leader should not just direct his men. He should try to understand them and the circumstances in which they are placed, and thus deal with issues appropriately. To this end, good communication skills and training methods are paramount.

The effectiveness of the leadership and communication skills displayed by the officers of the 1st Battalion leading up to the events of 21 September 1918 is of crucial significance. The part they played will later become more apparent.

HOW COURAGE IS SPENT

It is interesting to note that when publishing his observations, Lord Moran wrote some 55 pages on how best to bolster courage and resilience, but he devoted a great deal more space (90 pages) to his discussion of the numerous factors that can contribute to men not responding well to battlefront conditions.

Moran's observations are particularly relevant to the circumstances of the mutiny involving Australian soldiers that took place on the Western Front. In discussing the durability of 'courage', Moran summed it up bluntly by saying, 'Men wear out in war like clothes.'[5] Factors that can exacerbate this process include incessant artillery bombardments, exposure to severe weather conditions (in particular cold winters) and rising casualty rates.

In fact, as the casualty rates rose, the decline in morale and courage began to snowball, and a vicious circle came into existence. As stouthearted men were killed or incapacitated, they were replaced by inexperienced newcomers, and so the men who remained behind slowly but surely lost access to comrades upon whom they had relied and who may well have provided them with mental fortitude and an example to follow. As Lord Moran concluded, 'the stoutest-hearted men were lost; their numbers were replaceable, their spiritual worth never could be.'[6]

Other key courage-sapping factors listed by Lord Moran were fatigue, monotony and the death of comrades. He saw fatigue as the reason why some men seemed as though 'the sap had gone out of them, they are dried up.'[7] Anyone who has read diaries written by men on the Western Front will have been surprised to learn just how often monotony was a part of their daily lives. A monotonous and boring existence deprives men of a sense of anticipation, of something to look forward to. When such a situation exists amongst men who are far from home, it is not surprising that it has a role to play in dissipating courage.

Monotony lent itself to thought and introspection. Lord Moran felt that when men did think, it was unwise 'to live in the present ... that they should cheat their present distress by a flight into other times, away from all the tribulations of the passing hour.' The men who were most susceptible were those who spent lengthy periods of inactivity alone.[8] Bill Gammage recorded that Gallipoli diary entries revealed that 'above all, the monotony of their lives and the lack of progress [against the enemy] wore down the hopes of the Australians.' Even the officers were known to express despair as a result of their situation. Captain Ernest Warren wrote, 'The strain is gradually telling and if I stick it out for more than three months without a charge I will be agreeably surprised.'[9]

The men on the Western Front were confronted by death on a regular basis. It was when they considered and dwelt on those deaths that they were most vulnerable. To deal with this situation, the men at the front would, at times, joke about it or speak about it with derision. Moran recalled one incident in which a soldier, noticing that his comrade was 'off his feed', advised him that he 'had better eat it [his meal] up, it's as likely as not your last.' To another, he said, 'Cheer up, Cockie; it's your turn next.'[10] For some men, black humour was an essential part of dealing with the harsh reality.

This picture, taken at Vaire-Sur-Somme on 5 May 1918, shows not only laconic Australian humour, but also a common yearning for home. [AWM E04795]

Such examples of humour must be seen for what they were...'coping mechanisms', i.e., ways devised by the men themselves to deal with the horrors and realities of life on battlefields such as Gallipoli and the Western Front. One of the most discussed coping mechanisms was that of running away from it all; mutiny and desertion.

OFFICIAL PUNISHMENTS FOR DESERTION AND MUTINY

It is frequently stated that no Australian was executed for desertion or mutiny during World War I. However, this is not quite correct, as two Australians were executed for desertion, but both were serving as members of the New Zealand Expeditionary Force at the time. These men were John Joseph Sweeney, originally from Scottsdale in Tasmania, who enlisted in New Zealand, as he happened to be working there at the time, and Frank Julius Needs, who enlisted under the name of John King. Sweeney was 37 years old at the time of his death, and it is believed he was genuinely suffering from shellshock. His father committed suicide in 1925 upon learning the true circumstances surrounding his son's death. King gave his age as 29 when he enlisted, but he was actually believed to be considerably older. It is also said that he suffered from alcoholism. Both men were original Gallipoli Anzacs, and were two of only five men from the New Zealand Army who were executed during the Great War.[11]

Logically, it is not correct to classify these men as Australians, as they were not fighting in the Australian uniform. Less logically, some current writers say that Australians who were killed as early as August 1914 were the first Australian deaths of the Great War, despite the fact that they were wearing a British uniform and fighting with British military units.

It is also widely believed that Australian soldiers, unlike their British counterparts, were not subject to the death penalty for offences such as desertion and mutiny. Not so well known are the specifics of that determination. Similarly, it is believed that exempting Australians from the death penalty was right and proper, because the AIF was primarily a volunteer force. This latter view overlooks the fact that military conscription did not exist in Britain when the war began.

In an official report written after the war, Colonel Arthur Butler suggested that the real reasons why Australia's soldiers were treated differently related to Australia's historical development:

'The social injustices of the early history of Australia had bitten deeply into the national feelings and tradition, and subsequent history had not tended to lessen this. This was reflected in a demand for a more definitely moral perspective in the adjustment of punishment to crime ... The

Australian system of industrial arbitration, for example, was the most exact example hitherto to adjust relations ... In a word, Australia was constructively "democratic".'[12]

Butler was referring, in part, to the Australians' convict origins and the social turmoil of colonial Australia. In the early 20th century, the federal government's introduction of a basic wage was a groundbreaking development.

In fact, the relevant legislation for the Australian troops predated the war by some 11 years. Section 98 of the Australian Defence Act of 1903 stated:

'...no member of the Defence Force shall be sentenced to death by any court martial except for four offences: mutiny; desertion to the enemy; or traitorously delivering up to the enemy any garrison, fortress, post, guard, or ship, vessel or boat, or aircraft; or traitorous correspondence with the enemy.'

Significantly, this sentence could not be carried out until it was confirmed by the Governor-General.[13]

The key point being made here is that technically it was possible for Australians to face the firing squad if found guilty of mutiny or certain types of desertion, subject to the approval of the Governor-General. This point is particularly pertinent to an upcoming examination of the mutiny that occurred within the ranks of the AIF during the closing weeks of the Great War.

British generals tended to see the death penalty as a significant deterrent to desertion, and therefore a positive factor in maintaining military discipline. Not so widely recognised is the fact that a significant number, if not the vast majority, of Australian generals 'were at one with their British counterparts and Haig in particular.'[14] Even General John Monash, who later proved himself an astute observer of his men and their limitations, believed that the Australian government's refusal to allow the death penalty was bad for discipline. In mid-1917, he confirmed the death penalty for six men, but the sentences were later commuted to ten years of penal servitude. He believed that the execution of a small number of Australian men would act as a deterrent to anyone contemplating desertion. Rates of desertion among Australian troops were consistently higher than those among troops from other nations, and the absence of the death penalty was considered to be the reason for this.[15]

The problem for the military authorities lay in the fact that they had to maintain strict control over large numbers of men who could be ordered into horrific and life-threatening battle situations.

Historians such as Peter Stanley have pointed out that British generals were possibly quite correct in stating that the maintenance of strict military discipline over the Australian troops would have been more achievable had the death penalty existed as a deterrent. The five AIF divisions had the highest rate of criminal offences of any of the 60-plus British Empire divisions in France. By mid-1917, the rate of absence and desertion for the AIF divisions was four times greater than that of other divisions.[16]

> Photograph of a group of ten
> Australian deserters which was sent to the A.P.M.
> Havre, with the following letter:-
>
> "Sir,
>   With all due respect we send you this P.C.
> as a souvenir trusting that you will keep it as a
> mark of esteem from those who know you well. At the
> same time trusting that Nous jamais regardez vous
> encore. Au revoir.
>   Nous"

Ten unidentified Australian deserters. This picture was sent to the Assistant Provost Marshall GHQ as a souvenir for him with the message, 'We will never see you again.' [AWM A03862]

POLITICAL DEBATE

Throughout the war there was, at various times, a flurry of communication, both within the Australian military hierarchy and between them and the Australian government over the issue of capital punishment being used as a deterrent against mutiny and desertion. As the stalemate of the Western Front ground on and mortality rates rose, this issue became a focus of both public debate and government communiques.

Following a recommendation from Lieutenant General William Birdwood, Commander-in-Chief of the AIF, that Section 98 be waived, a formal request to introduce the death penalty was made to the Australian government on 9 July 1916. The government chose to delay its response, as it was planning a referendum on the issue of conscription. The result of the referendum, along with a sharp increase in the number casualties that occurred on the Somme at that time, meant that the British request was ultimately denied.

The matter resurfaced in April–May 1917 when the number of Australian deserters rose sharply. Monash approached Birdwood saying that even a limited number of executions would be a sufficient deterrent. As an alternative, Monash suggested that penal sentences imposed by courts martial be fully served even if the war ended before the sentence was complete. Birdwood well knew what the response of the Australian government would be, but he saw it as his role to try anyway. When the government duly rejected both options, Birdwood asked the Australian Defence Minister Senator George

Pearce 'to approve the publication in all Australian newspapers and in AIF orders of deserter's names, towns of enlistment and sentences.' Once again, this approach coincided with a conscription referendum and an increase in desertions and imprisonments...', leaving Pearce little choice but to agree to Birdwood's proposal, which came into effect in January 1918.'[17]

It is well known that at the start of the Great War, military authorities in general and medical authorities in particular had a lot to learn about how to deal with the mental and moral breakdown of some of the men in their charge. As the war progressed, it became apparent that learning how to deal with mental trauma such as shell-shock was no easy task. In fact, the term 'shell-shock' was not in common use prior to the First World War.

CHAPTER 5
DEALING WITH THE REALITIES

Start by doing what's necessary; then do what's possible; and suddenly you are doing the impossible.
Francis of Assisi

CHAPTER 5

DEALING WITH THE REALITIES

Start by doing what's necessary; then do what's possible; and suddenly you are doing the impossible.
Francis of Assisi

The Gallipoli campaign certainly brought the realities and horrors of war home to those who were part of it. Numerous individual accounts attest to the harsh realities that confronted the men during their eightmonth occupation of the peninsula. Just one month after the initial landing, Chaplain William Dexter, who had been helping to bury the dead, stated that 'the ground was simply covered with dead between the trenches' and 'the bodies were horrible to look at, being black and swelled up, stretching out the clothing.'[1] It was a military defeat, as it had failed to achieve its objective of pushing on to Constantinople; the only successful aspect had been the evacuation that had taken place without further loss of life.

As these realities filtered back home, the Australian government faced the unenviable task of dealing with a problem with which the soldier at the battlefront had already been confronted. Consequently, as the war continued through 1916 and into 1917, the Australian government faced a vastly different situation to that of the previous war years.

These years also witnessed a change in the government's approach to the war effort, which was reflected in the nature of the propaganda it used to encourage men to enlist and the public to contribute in some way. It began to rely more on the provisions of the War Precautions Act to maintain a focus on the war, both in terms of economic and industrial management and also in the minds of the people. There was also a change in the public's attitude towards the war in general. As the casualty lists grew, so too did the fear that they would soon include the name of a loved one or that of a neighbour or friend. The earlier enthusiasm of the most ardent supporters was diminishing, and opponents of the war were becoming more vocal. Germans and other aliens in Australia became the targets of abuse and mistrust. The numbers of eligible men persuaded to fight declined markedly. Enlistments fell from a high of 22,101 in January 1916 to 6170 in August of the same year. For the soldiers at the battlefront, especially those less able to cope with the horrors they faced, there was a consolidation and an amplification of coping mechanisms that had begun to appear.

The most obvious factor in the change that was taking place was the sharp rise in the number of casualties. One source gives the total number of Australian deaths in battle in the Dardanelles as 7818. During 1916, this figure increased by just over 60% to a total of 12,541 deaths, while in 1917 there was a further increase of 59% to a total of 20,036 deaths.[2]

These figures were horrendous, and were possibly unexpected. Current observers see these statistics as the outcome of employing battle tactics that were inappropriate for trench warfare and the new weapons of war. Australian soldiers, still reeling from the tribulations of Gallipoli, suffered appalling losses at Fromelles. Historians now know that this particular battle was doomed to fail even before it began because the Germans knew exactly what the British were attempting to do.

The growing casualty rates and the horrors of the war are directly reflected in the decline in enlistments in Australia. As stated earlier, the Australian government's promises were easily exceeded in 1914 with 52,561 enlistments, and support for the war effort, bolstered by the recruitment drives, remained high in 1915 with 165,912 enlistments, but 1916 saw a decline to

124,352 enlistments, followed by a substantial decline in 1917 to just 45,101 enlistments. The Commonwealth government had to find a way to deal with this situation, particularly in view of its habit of providing assurances, even making promises, to the British government.[3]

BOUND FOR THE WESTERN FRONT

The men of the 1st Battalion arrived in France in March 1916, including Rollo Taplin, who arrived in Marseilles on 28 March 1916 after travelling on HMT *Ivernia*. Having speculated that Rollo may have been striving to 'strike out on his own' rather than continuing to rely on his sister for accommodation and employment, it is also possible to speculate that once he had completed his training and arrived at an unfamiliar destination, he was keen to 'fit in' with his new companions and circumstances.

Now that he had arrived at the Western Front, he was in company with a large number of men, some of whom would also get caught up in the events of 21 September 1918.

One of those companions was Private James John Couley, whose military career thus far was very similar to that of Private Rollo Charles Taplin. Both men had enlisted in July 1915, with

Taplin signing on just eight days before Couley. Both men had received their training at the Liverpool camp, and both had been deployed as reinforcements for the 1st Battalion and were members of D Company.

However, the similarities ended there. Whereas Taplin was just 18 years and seven months old at the time of his enlistment, Couley was 32 years and ten months of age. Although both men were Australianborn and single, Rollo Taplin had spent most of his life living in Sydney, while James Couley had been born in Gulgong in NSW and was a shearer. Whereas Rollo Taplin was a devout Roman Catholic and quiet by nature, James Couley had been baptised into the Church of England and even before leaving Australia had incurred the wrath of military authorities because of his behaviour.[4]

While Rollo Taplin may have been keen to fit in with his comrades, it is unclear whether he deferred to James Couley as a mentor or simply saw him as a fellow soldier, albeit one whose behaviour he did not wish to emulate, for Couley's background and behaviour were vastly different to his own. In many ways, the differences between the two men were indicative of the differences between the 'old stagers' of 1914–1915 and the 'deep thinkers' of 1916–1918 that has been noted by Peter Stanley.

Of the men who travelled to the Western Front on board the *Ivernia*, 16 were later involved in the events of 21 September 1918, including four men who had fought at Gallipoli. Of these 16, ten were later to achieve the rank of Corporal or Lance Corporal. This latter group were to play a pivotal role in the events of the mutiny. One way to speculate on which, if any, of these men Rollo may have become close friends with is to select those who were similar in age or who had enlisted at approximately the same time.

Rollo Taplin. It is possible that this picture was taken on board the Ivernia as it headed for Marseilles.[Photo courtesy of the Taplin family].

Using this method, there are four men who were potentially friends of the young Australian soldier. These men were Lance Corporal Edward

Porter, a 21-year-old printer from Maitland in NSW, Corporal Reginald McKay, a 22-year-old tailor from Sydney, Lance Corporal Leonard Pettit, a 19-year-old labourer, also from Sydney, and Lance Corporal Cecil William Muir, an 18-year-old labourer from Newcastle in NSW. Of this group of four, the first three were members of C Company at the time of the mutiny, while Cecil Muir – along with Rollo Taplin – were members of D Company. Both of them were later to become Non-Commissioned Officers (NCOs) but at the time of arriving in Marseilles, all of them held the rank of private.

The military careers of Taplin and Muir were remarkably similar. Although a country boy, having been born in West Wallsend, near Newcastle in NSW, Muir had also enlisted in Liverpool. Both men rose to the rank of Lance Corporal and both men were subsequently charged with mutiny and desertion at the field courts martial that followed the events of 21 September 1918.

Also on board the *Ivernia* when it arrived in Marseilles on 28 March 1916 was Private David Watkin Humphreys. He was from Merewether in Newcastle and had enlisted at Liverpool on 28 July 1915, later rising to the rank of Lance Corporal. He faced the field courts martial in the same group of 34 men as Lance Corporal

Muir. Perhaps all three men were in the photograph above. Two other men who were tried among that group of 34 and who were both members of D Company and had arrived in France on board the *Ivernia* with Rollo Taplin were Private Alfred Woodford, a horse driver from Newtown, and Private Matthew Mackey, who had been born in Durham in England and had been working as a bread carter in Sydney when he enlisted.

Another man from D Company was Private William James Robson. He was almost the same age as Rollo Taplin and had also enlisted in July 1915. Robson had been born in Paddington in Sydney and had been a motor engineer and draughtsman. However, he had been sent to the battlefront much earlier than Rollo Taplin, having left Australia within a month of his enlistment and been deployed to Gallipoli.

There were four other Gallipoli men, all later involved in the mutiny, who travelled with Rollo on board the *Ivernia* to the Western Front. These men were Lance Corporal Ernest Besley from Sydney, Private Alan Barclay from Geelong in Victoria, Private Arthur Mullins from Moss Vale in NSW and Private Arthur Lawrence from Quirindi in NSW. Private Barclay had taken part in the original landings at Gallipoli. Of this group of four, only Besley was in D Company; the other three were in B Company. All four of these Gallipoli survivors were later to be caught up in the events of 21 September 1918. At age 31, Private Lawrence was the oldest member of this particular group of Gallipoli men. Key details of the military careers of Privates Mullins and Besley were outlined earlier. It is quite possible that Rollo Taplin became friendly with these young men, most of whom were of a similar age, but who already had battlefront experience.

On board the *Ivernia* when it arrived in Marseilles on 28 March 1916, but not involved in the mutiny, nor in the subsequent courts martial, was Jack Charles Hayes, who was a member of A Company. Hayes was involved, along with five others, in a deed of valour in August 1918, although this is not to imply that he was the only man among this group who was later to respond bravely. His particular deed of heroism was discussed at length by Charles Bean, who saw it as indicative of the fighting abilities of the men of the AIF. More significant is the fact that this deed has indirect relevance to the causes of the mutiny. When the daring of Hayes and his fellow comrades are later outlined, it will be seen why deeds such as this contributed to the development of a view that the men of the AIF were being asked to contribute more than their fair share because they dared to go when and where other troops hesitated to proceed.

While discussing heroic behaviour, there is one other relevant detail concerning this particular group of new arrivals to the Western Front. Among the men charged and imprisoned as a result of the mutiny of 21 September 1918 were three men who had been awarded the Military Medal for their gallantry. All three were on board the *Ivernia* when it arrived in Marseilles in March 1916. These men were Lance Corporal Ernest Walker, a 25-year-old tile layer from Sydney, Corporal Roger Cooney, a 21-year-old labourer from Brunswick in Victoria and Private James Couley, a 32-year-old shearer from Gulgong in NSW. All three men were to prove themselves capable of valour, but all three were also to prove themselves capable of larrikin behaviour.[5]

None of these men from the 1st Battalion who had arrived on the *Ivernia* were involved in the dreadful fighting that took place at Fromelles. It was the men of the 5th Battalion who were subject to the vicious slaughter that took place there. This fighting marked Australia's introduction to the Western Front. As part of the 1st Division, the men of the 1st Battalion entered the line on 23 July 1916, in the assault on the small village of Pozieres in the Somme Valley.

Given that this was Rollo Taplin's first involvement in the war, it was certainly a case of being 'thrown in at the deep end'. Pozieres became the centre of some extremely vicious and costly fighting. It was initially captured by the 1st Division on 23 July, and by the time they were relieved on 27 July, they had suffered some 5285 casualties.

Men from the 1st Battalion were involved in the bloody fighting that took place in and around Pozieres from 27 July to 3 September 1916. Even Charles Bean, who had been at Gallipoli and witnessed all its horrors, was shocked by what he saw at Pozieres. He wrote about the conditions faced by the men, but more importantly, in terms of what was to occur later in the war, he wrote about the attitudes the men in the trenches were forming towards their commanders. Many were seriously, but usually silently, questioning the wisdom of their command decisions. One Lance Corporal wrote, 'I should never have got out alive.'[6] Another told of how there were 'brains hanging out, heads bashed in, arms and legs apart from bodies.'[7] Some felt that too often, relatively unimportant objectives were gained as the result of excessive strain and losses. Bean noted that 'the prevailing tactics [which involved] repeated shallow advances on narrow fronts were dreaded and detested ...

it is not surprising [that] ... some intelligent men [felt] ... that they were being uselessly sacrificed.'[8]

The horror of war; no-man's-land on the Western Front, 2 September 1918. [AWM E03149]

Another observer who provided an extensive but seldom critical commentary throughout his lengthy war service was Archie Barwick, who was a member of C Company, 1st Battalion. Barwick was a Gallipoli veteran, and he too had arrived in Marseilles on board the *Ivernia*, albeit ten days earlier than Rollo Taplin and his comrades. Extracts from Barwick's extensive wartime diaries were published in 2013, and it is interesting to note the similarities between his service record on the Western Front and that of Rollo Taplin. Both men were to receive promotions, both were sent to training schools at various times and both were hospitalised with wounds. Archie Barwick was ultimately promoted to the rank of sergeant and was awarded the Croix de Guerre by the King of Belgium. Archie was not caught up in the events of 21 September 1918, as he had been wounded for the third time in April of that year, and after an absence of more than three months because of his wounds and an illness, he was placed on the supernumerary list.

Recording his experiences at Pozieres, on 24 July 1916 he wrote, 'Men were being buried by the dozen, but were frantically dug out again, some dead and some alive.'[9] Archie Barwick also provided an insight into the pride in their achievements that had slowly been developing within the AIF. On 27 July 1916, he wrote:

'The colonel lined us all up and for the first time in his life he reckoned we had done a marvellous thing; how he praised us. He said we had now, by taking this Pozieres Wood after the English had twice failed to take it, covered ourselves and Australia with glory, and we had upheld the old Gallipoli reputation....'[10]

This record indicates that at least some Australian officers were well aware of the positive impact that praise had on boosting morale. It is also an indication of the early development of the Gallipoli legend. The colonel's remark may well have been based on his perception of the facts, but in reality the AIF were to prove most effective when supported by experienced troops from other countries, especially Britain.

Whatever the circumstances, the outcome was that Rollo Taplin was admitted to an Anzac Rest Station on 19 August 1916 suffering from a new phenomenon known as 'shell-shock'. Respite, however, was brief, as he was discharged just four days later so he could rejoin his battalion. In that same month, Archie Barwick was promoted to the rank of corporal. He had received his promotion to lance corporal just two months earlier, and two months later was promoted, in the field, to the rank of sergeant. Rapid promotions such as these were not uncommon, and were indicative of the rate of attrition among frontline troops at that time.

Rollo Taplin remained with his battalion in the field until 2 December 1916, when he was sent off for a fortnight's training at the Lewis Machine Gun School of Instruction. During this period of training, it is reasonable to assume that he would have made some new friends. It is even more likely that during his time away from the front line he yearned for a safe return to his sister and other family members and friends back in Australia. Time spent away from the battalion always had the potential to weaken each individual's sense of belonging. This particular period of leave occurred not long after the first of the two conscription referendums, which had been held on 28 October 1916. Rollo returned to his battalion on 17 December 1916.[11]

Of the 17 months that had passed since he had enlisted, Rollo Taplin had spent about eight months training in Australia and then being transported to the Western Front. Some of his training had occurred after he had left Australia, and in this he was no different to many of his comrades who had travelled the same path before him. His service record suggests that his experiences on the Western Front were very similar in some ways to those of other members of the 1st Battalion who had preceded him, men who had been put into boats and landed at Gallipoli under cover of darkness. He had arrived in France just in time to become caught up in some of the most horrendous fighting witnessed on the Western Front.

This was happening to a young man, not yet 19 years old, who at an early age had been required to take responsibility for an extensive brood of younger half-siblings, only to later be abandoned by his father and directed to the nearest orphanage. He was now fighting alongside other young Australian men, some of whom would have been overwhelmed by their new circumstances. Some of these men reacted stoically, either because of their character or their training, or a combination of both, while others reacted in an entirely different fashion.

GOVERNMENT RESPONSE TO DECLINING ENLISTMENT

As enlistments declined, the Australian government began to turn its attention towards the issue of conscription for military service overseas. Under the Defence Act of 1903, they already possessed the power to conscript men for military service within Australia. However, Prime Minister Billy Hughes did not have public support, nor support from within the parliament, to introduce conscription for overseas service, and so he now sought this approval. Hughes had been told by British military authorities that 16,500 new recruits were needed each month to offset the losses that were occurring on the Western Front, and he was determined to accommodate that request. There were groups within the community who supported Hughes's position. One such group was the Universal Service League, which had been formed in 1915.

Other groups included the Women's Christian Temperance Union and the National Council of Women.

It is well known that this particular issue, perhaps more than any other in our history, split the community. Groups such as the Women's Peace Army, who opposed involvement in the war as well as conscription, were vehement in their opposition. Other groups, such as the Australian Railways Union, supported the war effort but were strongly opposed to conscription. The campaigns waged by both sides preceded two referendums that were held on 28 October 1916 and 20 December 1917. On both occasions, those who campaigned in favour of a 'No' vote were victorious, but only by a narrow margin, although that margin increased in the second referendum.

The men at the front line were given the opportunity to cast a vote on the conscription issue, and it is interesting to learn how they voted. Some voted for conscription in the belief that unless adequate reinforcements arrived to assist them, their chances of returning to their loved ones would be greatly reduced. Others saw a 'Yes' vote as a continuation of support from those back in Australia. This was how Archie Barwick saw it, for when he learnt that the 'No' vote for the second referendum had prevailed by a margin of 200,000, he wrote in his diary, 'If this is true ... it practically means that the people of Australia are not behind us....' He went on to say that he felt ashamed of his country for not supporting the men at the front.[12] Conversely, other soldiers felt that no one should be forcibly subjected to the horrors that they themselves had faced. During the first referendum, the federal government published a letter supporting conscription that had supposedly been written by VC winner Bert Jacka. His father was incensed, and swore a statutory declaration that his son was opposed to conscription, but the government censors refused to allow his declaration to be published.[13]

The conscription referendums are not the central focus here, but they are relevant, and so it is necessary to be aware of them and the manner in which they divided Australian opinion on the war and how best to deal with it. The referendums also showed how the government continued to see propaganda as a means of manipulating public opinion throughout the war. The government was sufficiently astute to realise that following the bloodshed and horrible realities of battles such as Fromelles and Passchendaele, it needed to alter the focus of its campaigns. As far as the men who were already serving were concerned, the focus had subtly shifted from one of patriotic love of country to one of standing by and remaining loyal to one's fellow soldiers.

It was during the controversy generated by the conscription referendums that the British military authorities pressed the Australian government to change its policy on execution as a deterrent to desertion. Some senior Australian officers also aired their views that Australia should cease its refusal to execute deserters.

Ever mindful of the need to avoid any further aggravation of their constituents, the Australian government resisted these calls to change its policy regarding the use of capital punishment as a deterrent to desertion. However, some concessions were granted, and it was belatedly agreed that the names of those found guilty of desertion would be published for all to see.

Much more immediate and also more effective was the decision that was made as to how the military authorities were to deal with soldiers going AWL. It was realised that, on some occasions, soldiers who had gone AWL had done so to avoid front-line duty. If these men were then taken from the front line to be subjected to a court martial and imprisoned, their time away from the battlefront would be lengthened, meaning that the malingerers would have effectively achieved the outcome they were seeking. This situation was not to be allowed to continue. Thus, it was decided that the men were to be charged expeditiously and then returned to their units as quickly as possible. The Australian government finally gave way and adopted an option put forward by Major General John Monash. Any penal sentence imposed by a court martial was to be served in full, even if the war had ended in the meantime.

MEDICAL AUTHORITIES AND MEDICAL TRAUMA

At the same time, there was somewhat of a softening of the attitude by Australian generals towards those who were genuinely suffering from shell-shock. However, this change in attitude was a long time in coming, and did not really emerge until towards the end of 1917. In December 1917, Lieutenant General William Birdwood, Commander of I ANZAC Corps 1916–1917, conceded that some breakdowns were very different to deliberate cases of desertion. By July 1918, when John Monash had succeeded Birdwood, Australian officers were being instructed not just to read the court records of men found guilty of desertion, but also to consider the men's personal records. The official number of men from the First AIF who were discharged from service from all fronts due to war-related psychological trauma was 4984.[14] There is little doubt that this official figure understates the number of men who were actually suffering from psychological trauma.

It is possible that the changing attitude towards and treatment of psychological pain and suffering caused by the horrendous conditions on the Western Front was the area in which medical knowledge achieved its most significant advances. That changes were made is undeniable, but many would say that even for that time, these changes did not go far enough. There were many whose symptoms of mental trauma were suppressed, and others whose symptoms did not become known until after the war had ended. Men given inadequate treatment during the war were all too often left to flounder after its conclusion. This is certainly a view brought forward in Alastair Thompson's book *Anzac Memories: Living with the Legend*. His study discusses issues that arose within his own family, stemming from the post-war psychological problems of his grandfather Hector Thompson. Alastair Thompson went on to study several other similar cases, and how the Australian government responded to them.

For 1914 and most of 1915, many psychological or mental breakdowns on the battlefield were regarded with considerable scepticism, or referred to as 'hysteria' or the vague concept of 'neurasthenia'. It is not known for sure whether the term 'shell-shock' derived from the medical service or from the men themselves, but it is generally accepted that it was better understood by the French Army than by the British Army. It was not until the latter months of the Gallipoli campaign that people came to accept that shell-shock was a genuine condition and that its treatment should invariably involve the evacuation of the sufferer. Colonel Arthur Butler (AAMC) recorded:

> '...the acceptance of "shock" (or in the later months of the [Gallipoli] campaign, "shell-shock", (a term that certainly came to Gallipoli from France) as a major element in the aetiology of cases.'[15]

Military authorities also recognised that the existence of this medical condition was very much dependent upon the morale of a company or battalion. Thus, it was seen as productive to remove men who were suffering from shell-shock from their unit until they could be sent back to the front. However, it still took some time before the British army officially accepted that there was a link between the trauma of battle and shell-shock.

An army order was issued early in 1916 stating that 'these cases when associated with "enemy action" were [to be] returned as "wounded", not "sick".' This was new ground for medical authorities. Understandably, there were those who had reservations about this new approach. They felt that some men who were suffering from simple strain or lack of sleep had been diagnosed as suffering from shell-shock. Initially, the British only recognised shell-shock as a symptom stemming from an injury to the brain. In 1915, they decided that any man presenting with symptoms of shell-shock that had been caused by the enemy, for example, following heavy bombardment, would be classified as wounded. However, if the man's mental breakdown did not follow a shell explosion, this breakdown was not thought to be due to the enemy, and thus the man was to be classified as sick. Consequently, that man was not entitled to a wound stripe or a pension.[16]

Alastair Thompson commented at length on the injustice of this decision. His book *Anzac Memories: Living with the Legend* details a number of cases wherein former members of the AIF who were suffering from post-war psychological problems were forced to fight a long and difficult battle with the Australian government to obtain some level of assistance.

COPING MECHANISMS

The soldier at the battlefront still had to deal with the situation he faced. He may well have been unaware of the slowly evolving medical approaches and attitudes concerning the trauma of battle, but he still needed to develop, either consciously or instinctively, ways of surviving the horrors around him. Each individual had to deal with his current situation. There were a number of ways to achieve this and, collectively, the methods used will be referred to as 'coping mechanisms'.

The soldiers on the Western Front were given no opportunity to debate the conscription issue with Australian politicians, but they did get the chance to cast a vote on the matter. Interestingly votes cast by the AIF members from the battlefields were neither decisively in favour of the introduction of conscription nor strongly against it. In both referendums, the vote from the serving soldiers was in favour of conscription, but not overwhelmingly so. It is difficult to identify the individual viewpoints of the men at the time of each referendum because of government censorship of letters sent back home, but the men at the battlefront tended to put on a brave face. They were more likely to reassure their loved ones that all was well, despite the fact that this was not always so.

The soldier on the battlefield had to get on with it or get away from it. Some inventive methods were used to 'get away from it' (the battle field). In fact, it was even suggested that some men had enlisted knowing full well that they may later be considered unfit for battlefront duty. Even before the convoy set off from Egypt for Gallipoli, Australian medical authorities were given the task of weeding out those men 'unlikely to prove efficient soldiers ... Among them were a considerable number who had got into the force by concealing disease, knowing they could compel discharge at any time by disclosing it.'[17]

Being wounded or incurring an illness of some significance could lead to the sufferer being removed from the front line, if not permanently, then at least temporarily. For some men, the best way to achieve this was the self-inflicted wound (SIW). Anyone in the British army found guilty of inflicting a wound upon themselves could be executed. Some 3894 British soldiers were found guilty of SIWs, although none of them were actually executed.[18] Numerous SIWs were detected at Gallipoli, and the reactions of the comrades of those who took this drastic action were mixed. Most could understand why they would do it, and many pitied those who they had resorted to such measures. However, there were also occasions when such men were treated with disdain and contempt.

Alf Stabb, of the 29th Battalion, was at a casualty clearing station on the Western Front in April 1918 when a shell exploded nearby, inflicting minor wounds to his right hand. He was quickly bandaged and then placed on a stretcher near two other men who also had hand wounds. He was puzzled as to why the medical orderlies then proceeded to ignore all three men. When a doctor later appeared and questioned the three of them, it became apparent that the other two men were suffering from SIWs, and it had been assumed that because his injury was similar, Alf's wound was also self-inflicted.[19]

The British military authorities were determined to reduce the numbers of men inflicting injuries upon themselves, because such matters were taken very seriously. At the end of the war, when war gratuities (money in addition to the men's normal pay based on length of service) were being allocated, it was determined that men who had been convicted of SIWs, along with deserters and men who had been dishonourably discharged, as well as men serving a sentence in excess of 12 months following a court martial, would not receive any gratuity.[20]

Some men took extreme measures to administer an SIW. Ern Morton recalled being repeatedly pestered by a fellow soldier at Gallipoli to break his arm for him. Men used the picks with which they tunnelled under the enemy trenches to stab themselves in the leg. Another trick was to put condensed milk on their penis and claim that they were suffering from a venereal disease. One of Ern Morton's experiences led to a significant change in his outlook. He encountered a young, mortally wounded German officer who begged him, in fluent English, to end his suffering. Morton was stunned; from that moment on, he refused to fire a shot at the enemy, and became a staunch advocate for the 'No' vote in the conscription referendum.[21]

However, the men's reactions were not always so passive, and frustration was occasionally vented against the authorities. This could take the form of derisive comments about their officers made behind their backs or, on certain occasions, much more obvious expressions of distaste. There was an occasion back in Australia when Prime Minister Billy Hughes, whilst campaigning in favour of conscription, had eggs thrown at him by members of the public. Similarly, towards the end of the war, Australian soldier Fred Farrall recalled how an unnamed general who had just finished telling his men that they might have to be returned to the front line was forced to leave hurriedly when some clods of dirt were thrown in the direction of his horse.[22]

Men understandably developed a sense of fatalism, a belief that they should 'just get on with it', and that 'what will be, will be'. On 15 October 1915, Lieutenant Robert Hunter, a solicitor from Forbes in NSW, wrote in his diary, 'What is it to me, if I am killed? I am not left to worry over it.' Tragically, he was killed in action on 13 June 1916, and later buried in a military cemetery at Wye Farm, south of Armentieres. Lieutenant Hunter, a devout Christian, had believed that 'war is sent with a purpose by God.' He later recorded how 'men, who months ago, would have been ashamed to have it known that they had a bible [and] are seen reading it often....'[23]

Some men put their faith in God and firmly believed that divine intervention would keep them in good stead. Lieutenant Eric Chinner, a bank clerk from Peterborough in South Australia, wrote in his diary, 'I feel sure God will watch over me. Cheerio anyway.' He later died in the German trenches trying to smother a bomb he had dropped.[24] Others turned to gambling or, when available, alcohol and/or prostitutes. For many, black humour gave them a sense of 'normality'. They would joke about death or find humour in the most unlikely situations. Bill Gammage recounted an incident in which a Private Grubb and his mate were cooking a meal amid heavy enemy shelling. 'We would cut an onion and then duck back into the dugout for our lives, then out again to give it a stir and in again as a shell came whistling by ... we were laughing all through because it was comical.'[25] Archie Barwick recalled that when they had sailed away from Australia, one of the men had joked that all the men of the 1st Division would be able to return to Australia in a row boat. As there were only four men left from his original H company, he felt that his prediction was fast coming true.[26] Such strategies were not peculiar to the Australian soldier; they existed in all armies on both sides of no-man's-land.

The military authorities were well aware of these coping mechanisms, but not so adept in alleviating the horrible situations that led to their existence. They did, however, attempt to catalogue them and compile statistics relevant to them. There would have been times when it was hard to say whether or not a wound was self-inflicted. Statistics were kept for both SIWs and accidental injuries. Not surprisingly, the numbers of both grew as the war dragged on.

Official SIWs for the AIF in France and Flanders increased from 126 in 1916 to 186 the following year and 388 in 1918. Accidental injuries more than doubled between 1916 and 1917, and then quadrupled to 2588 in 1918.[27]

No reliable statistics remain regarding suicides by members of the AIF during the war years, but men did take their own life as a result of the stresses they were under. Suicide was a recognised but often unreported phenomenon. On occasions, their comrades could never be sure whether the digger who had been shot by a sniper after raising his head above the parapet of the trench had done so deliberately or accidentally.

CHAPTER 6
MUTINY AND DESERTION

What lies behind you and what lies in front of you, pales in comparison to what lies inside of you.
Ralph Waldo Emerson

CHAPTER 6

MUTINY AND DESERTION

What lies behind you and what lies in front of you, pales in comparison to what lies inside of you. Ralph Waldo Emerson

The best-known mutiny associated with the history of Europeans in the Pacific region took place in 1787, at about the same time that Governor Phillip was getting ready to establish a convict settlement at Botany Bay. Captain Bligh was evicted from his vessel, the *Bounty*, and cast adrift in a longboat. Less than two decades later, he was appointed governor of the penal colony of NSW. This mutiny is very well known, and has been the subject of many books and several feature films. It might seem that this was Australia's only mutiny, particularly if the definition of these events excludes such incidents as the Eureka rebellion, which some see as a revolt against an oppressive mining tax.

However, the events of 21 September 1918, which involved men from the 1st Battalion AIF, were indeed mutinous, even if the men involved were only found guilty of desertion and acquitted of the charge of mutiny. The 1st Battalion mutiny is known only to a few, and has been ignored by all but a handful, but there is no denying that it did occur, and that it was the most significant mutiny of the First World War involving men from the AIF. With this mutiny, as with others, it is also very easy to take sides; to either condemn those who took part for their actions or, alternatively, to sympathise with them and feel that they were treated shabbily. Having examined the battle experiences of the men of the 1st Battalion and the personal backgrounds of some of the men who were later to take part in a mutiny, it is relevant to also examine just what forms of behaviour can be viewed as mutinous.

As had been the case throughout history, all armies involved in the Great War experienced instances of desertion, which basically involves leaving an appointed post. This problem could take a variety of forms, as some infringements that were recorded as being AWL were, in reality, cases of desertion. The men of the AIF were in a different situation to those of most nations, due in part to the effective absence of the death penalty for all disciplinary infringements aside from four specified offences subject to the approval of the GovernorGeneral. There is no doubt that instances of desertion, whether or not they were recorded as being AWL, were a serious cause of concern for military leaders. They caused a significant reduction in the availability of trained personnel, and were also a potential factor in lowering morale among the remaining soldiers.

Commanding officers also had to deal with the problem of mutiny. This involved men refusing to obey a specific order or refusing to tolerate conditions that they no longer found acceptable. All nations that fought in the Great War had to deal with this problem, some more so than others. Mutinies erupted within armies, as well as naval forces. It is possible to account for these mutinies both in terms of the circumstances that led up to them and in terms of the cultural background of each particular nation.

If armies are the products of societies, which are known to differ, then soldiers' reactions to war will also differ. Protest was more common in the AIF than it was in comparable forces. On one occasion when Archie Barwick and his comrades were having a bath in Etaples, an incident occurred that he believed underlined how unquestioning of authority the British Tommy (soldier) could be in comparison to the Australian soldier. He and his friends were told that they were to get a clean change of clothing, but were dismayed to find that the replacement clothes were just as filthy as the ones they had just discarded. The Australians decided to seek out an officer and insist that he lodge a complaint on their behalf. Archie wrote in his diary that some Tommies standing nearby were aghast at the reaction of the Australians, and concluded that they were more likely 'to take anything that's given them and ask no questions.'[1]

Conversely, it can be argued that no single protest or mutiny from within the AIF had as detrimental an impact on military effectiveness as, for example, some of those that occurred within the French army. The level of discipline deriving from the military training of the men is related to the severity of the punishments for mutiny. Also relevant are the particular circumstances existing at that particular time that led to the mutiny. Mutinies that occurred at critical times, such as when the enemy was on the attack, were probably dealt with more harshly.

There were a small number of mutinies involving men of the AIF during the First World War. In this, Australia was no different from many other nations involved in the war. Not all of these mutinies arose because the men refused to follow orders to go into battle. This particular kind of mutiny has sometimes been called a 'refusal mutiny', which is what occurs when men walk 'away from the line' (refuse to go into battle) by disobeying a direct order. It is highly likely that some such mutinies occurred as a result of fear and apprehension about what might occur on the battlefield. Commanding officers often tended to regard men who were involved in such mutinies as 'shirkers', or even cowards. Some may well have been shirkers, while others took part because there had been a breakdown in their resilience. This latter group could even include men who had fought bravely on previous occasions. There is little doubt that peer pressure would have played a significant part in a man's decision to refuse to go into battle. Accurately identifying which background factors are most relevant is an extremely difficult task, and can best be approached by examining a man's previous performance prior to his taking part in a mutiny. The background circumstances and context in which the mutiny occurred also need to be examined.

WARTIME MUTINIES

Many Australian soldiers who were found guilty of desertion and gaoled had committed crimes that were basically identical to some of those committed by their British counterparts, for whom the penalty had been death. In all likelihood, some Australian soldiers may not have deserted if the death penalty had been invoked.

It is possible to identify three different types of mutiny in terms of the situations from which they arose; 'industrial', 'disbandment' and 'refusal' mutinies. Australians were involved in instances of all three. Almost all the mutinies involving the AIF occurred during September 1918, when the war was drawing to a close. As the war had been dragging on for four long years, such a situation is hardly surprising.

However, another mutiny involving men from the AIF occurred in February 1916, well away from the battlefront.

INDUSTRIAL MUTINIES

'Industrial' mutinies usually occur as the result of conditions that are deemed to be intolerable. Those conditions have often been in place for some time, and despite grumblings and protestations, few or no improvements have been made. This is the underlying cause, and eventually, because reforms have not occurred or because people's personal safety and rights have been infringed, an outbreak of violence can occur. This outbreak comes as the result of a 'spark' that ignites an inflamed situation. Often, the spark can seemingly be unrelated to the long-term grievances.

Such a situation occurred in February 1916 at the Casula training camp near Liverpool, south-west of Sydney. The relevant background situation involved a group of army volunteers who had not yet fully come to terms with the rigours of army discipline. Some recruits were told that their training session was to be extended, and they refused to do the extra duty. They marched out of camp, heading towards Liverpool, and were joined by a large number of protesters. After invading local hotels, alcohol became a significant factor. Windows were smashed and trains commandeered. Trouble then erupted at Central Station where armed military guards became involved. When a shot was fired over their heads, the guards returned fire, killing one soldier, Ernest Keefe, and injuring eight others. After order was finally restored, about 30 soldiers were court-martialled and either gaoled or discharged. Ultimately, many of these men were still sent overseas to fight. The government was very keen to minimise damage to their recruitment efforts.

Interestingly, a group of convalescing diggers, who had recently returned from Gallipoli and were nearby when the riot occurred, condemned the actions of the rioters. They questioned their readiness to fight, given their reaction to a small increase in working hours.[2] Their response is further evidence of Peter Stanley's views regarding the differing outlook and background of many of those who fought in 1914–1915 compared with those who were sent to the front in later years.

Another mutiny involving members of the AIF and training camp conditions occurred in 1916 in Etaples in France. Here, harsh training camp conditions were exacerbated by training officers being dubbed 'canaries' because they wore yellow brassards and being perceived as not having any experience on the battlefront. Battle-weary veterans who had been sent there for training in gas warfare resented their methods. Trouble first erupted in August 1916 and involved members of the AIF and New Zealand Expeditionary Force (NZEF), four of whom were found guilty and sentenced to death. New Zealand-born and serving with the NZEF, Private Jack Braithwaite, who had worked as a journalist in Australia, was executed in October of that year, while the other three men had their sentences commuted. Trouble again erupted in September 1917, and during the ensuing riots a British corporal was shot and killed. At the end of the trouble, another British corporal, Jesse Robert Short, was executed and three others were sentenced to ten years of servitude. In his poem *Base Details,* poet Siegfried Sassoon was scathing towards the leadership at the camp:

> 'If I were fierce and bald and short of breath,
> I'd live with scarlet Majors at the Base,
> And speed glum heroes to their death.
> You'd see with my puffy petulant face,
> Guzzling and gulping in the best hotel,
> Reading the Roll of Honour, "Poor young chap",
> I'd say—"I used to know his father well:
> Yes, we've lost heavily in the last scrap."
> And when the war is done and the youth stone dead
> I'd toddle home safely and die ... in bed.'[3]

DISBANDMENT MUTINIES

Most of the mutinies involving the AIF and those that involved the greatest number of Australian participants occurred in September 1918 and were seen then, and are still seen today, as vastly different from the two outbreaks of violence reported above. These mutinies are often referred to as the 'disbandment' mutinies, and arose as the result of efforts to implement a form of consolidation of specific battalions whose numbers had declined substantially. It was estimated that because of a lack of reinforcements, the 57 Australian battalions were some 8500 men short in total. Thus, the military authorities decided to disband some battalions and transfer the remaining men to other battalions. A similar position had arisen for the British, French and German armies, and in each case the same solution was put forward.

The situation for the Australian battalions was made even more complicated by a decision to send the '1914 men' back to Australia on leave. Consequently, on 23 September the order was issued for the immediate disbandment of the 19th, 21st, 25th, 37th, 42nd, 54th and 60th Battalions. Rumours had been circulating for some time that disbandments were to occur, and this may well have influenced the thinking of the men in the 1st Battalion. While the officers and men of the designated battalions saw the overall need to implement this measure, they did not condone the selection of their particular battalions for disbandment. The men were fiercely loyal to their comrades, and thus refused to heed the disbandment order. These mutinies are of some relevance to the circumstances of the refusal mutiny, because they occurred almost simultaneously. Those who took part were well organised. They appointed their own officers, maintained military discipline and even organised a church parade. They had widespread support from members of other units of the AIF.

Ultimately, the situation was contained by virtue of the fact that General Monash postponed the order until after an upcoming attack on the Hindenburg Line. Technically, the actions of the Australians constituted a mutiny, but no military authority ever took any action against the men, and no charges were laid.[4]

The disbandment mutinies were given extensive coverage by Charles Bean. He was sympathetic towards them, as he saw the men's actions as a reflection of his view of the ideal Australian soldier as one who was fiercely loyal to his mates. They were exhibiting 'a public loyalty ... sustained with a flaming zeal, disconcerting to those who had encouraged it.'[5]

During the disbandment process, there was an interesting incident that involved Brigadier General Harold 'Pompey' Elliott. A decision had been made to transfer men from the 60th Battalion to the severely weakened 50th Battalion. This arrangement was to be formalised at a parade held on 26 September 1918, but the men refused to comply. Upon hearing about the plan to disobey the disbandment orders, Pompey

Elliott initially reacted angrily, telling the men that he was not going to allow them to become a mob, and pointing out to them that the death penalty could be invoked. The men were left in no doubt as to the degree of his anger, and one of the dissenters called out, 'We've got bullets too.' Following this remark, Elliott changed tack and decided to reason with them. He explained to them why the amalgamations were necessary and appealed to their better judgement. He also gave them half an hour to reconsider their position. Ultimately, after a short continuance of the discussion, the men relented and decided to move to their new units.[6]

REFUSAL MUTINIES

The most damaging mutinies were those that arose when men walked 'out of the line', or at least threatened to do so. Three of these involved Australian soldiers, and all three occurred late in the war, in September 1918, after a period of intense fighting. This would suggest that 'war weariness' was a key ingredient, but it was not the only factor. At the time of their occurrence, it was no certainty that the war was about to end, indeed the allied planners expected the war to continue into 1919, and planning was underway to deal with that eventuality should it occur.

The first recorded instance of a 'refusal' mutiny involving members of the AIF occurred near Peronne on 5 September 1918, just two weeks prior to an even larger mutiny. There were a lot of similarities between this mutiny and the mutiny on the Western Front of 21 September 1918. The men had just completed a period of sustained action and had moved to a rest area when they were again ordered up to the front line. Three platoons of B Company and a small number from A Company of the 59th Battalion were involved. The men complained to their officers that they were exhausted, and felt that they were being exploited by being asked to do more than their fair share.

Their brigade commander, Pompey Elliott, was able to persuade the men to reconsider, which they did, before rejoining the battalion. No charges arose from this incident.[7] Elliott had dealt with this problem in a very clever and tactful manner. He asked the men to write down their grievances, and then left, giving them time to think things over (and cool down). He even offered to speak on their behalf if they went ahead and the affair was investigated.[8] In other words, he was making it apparent that he saw their point of view, and yet at the same time ensuring that he got them 'back on track', the outcome he had been seeking.

A third mutiny occurred just four days after the mutiny of 21 September 1918 that also involved men refusing to go into the line. On 25th September, 13 men from the 3rd Australian Tunnelling Company refused to go forward to the line. They were charged with mutiny and appeared before a court martial, receiving sentences ranging from one to two years' imprisonment with hard labour.[9]

Charles Bean reported that 'there had during this period been slighter incidents, of which only hints are given in the records.'[10] This was all he had to say about them, claiming that he had no direct knowledge of these mutinies. Perhaps such behaviour was not in keeping with the image he had been fostering of the Australian soldier.

The second of the three refusal mutinies that occurred in September 1918 was the mutiny on the Western Front that occurred on 21 September 1918. This was the mutiny that involved the largest number of participants, with more than 115 men involved. Furthermore, the punishments meted out to those found guilty at the subsequent courts martial were more severe than those imposed following the other two refusal mutinies of September 1918. The men who took part received prison terms ranging from two years to three years for privates and five years to ten years for NCOs. In order to better understand why this particular refusal mutiny occurred, considerable background information has already been presented, including the personal stories of some of the mutineers. With the exception of Rollo Taplin, these personal stories have been gleaned solely from the men's service records.

Relevant background information regarding this particular mutiny has also included an outline of the contribution made by members of the 1st Battalion to the allied war effort. Ultimately, the purpose is to better understand why the mutineers reacted in such a manner. During this narrative further personal stories of some individual mutineers, derived from personal service records, will unfold. Looking at the bigger picture, it is also relevant to briefly trace the battlefield activities of the 1st Battalion.

THE 1st BATTALION ON THE WESTERN FRONT, 1917–1918

During the course of 1917, a further 76,836 Australians became casualties of the Great War. These casualties occurred on the Western Front, in places such as Bullecourt, Messines and, over a fourmonth period, around Ypres, in what became known as the Battle of Passchendaele.[11]

From 3 May until 17 May 1917, the 1st Battalion was involved in the second Battle of Bullecourt. During this battle, the Australians were able to penetrate the German lines, but further advances were frustrated. A series of determined German counterattacks proved costly in terms of Australian casualties. Ultimately, the Germans withdrew from the village, which in reality was of little strategic importance. Casualties among the three divisions of the AIF that were involved totalled 7482 men.

It was during the fierce fighting at Bullecourt that Corporal George Julian Howell of the 1st Battalion was awarded the VC, thereby becoming the third recipient of the award in the battalion. He had previously been wounded at Pozieres in 1916 and had been awarded the Military Medal for his actions at Dernancourt. His citation for the VC stated that:

'Howell, on his own initiative, single-handed and exposed to heavy bomb and rifle fire, climbed on top of the parapet and proceeded to bomb the enemy, pressing them back along the trench from where he greatly inspired them [his comrades] in the subsequent successful counter-attack.'

The fact that he spent several months in hospital recovering from wounds sustained during this action is further testimony to his valour. It also underlines the ferocity of the fighting.[12]

The I ANZAC Corps, of which the men of the 1st Division were a part, fought in the Third Battle of Ypres in Belgium between September and November 1917. In addition, individual actions that involved some but not all of the battalions within a division took place at Menin Road, Polygon Wood, Broodseinde, Poelcappelle and Passchendaele. Over the course of one eight-week period, the Australian forces suffered 38,000 casualties.[13] During the Third Battle of Ypres, some members of the 1st Battalion fought in and around the village of Broodseinde on 4 October 1917. The result was a significant defeat for the German army, which allowed the Allies to occupy all of the ridge south of the Passchendaele sector. Men from the 1st Battalion were again involved in the closing skirmishes of the Third Battle of Ypres in the Passchendaele sector from 26 October to 10 November 1917.

During this period of fighting, the Australian Light Horse, led by General Harry Chauvel, successfully captured Beersheba in Palestine. It is possible that news of this successful cavalry charge boosted the morale of the Australians on the Western Front, even if only briefly. Not so encouraging for them was the overthrow of the Russian monarchy, which meant that the Germans would soon be able to redeploy troops from the Eastern Front to the Western Front. On balance, it can be said that the fighting that took place during 1917, while extremely bloody and fierce, was of little benefit to the Allies. Historian Jonathan King recorded that 'Haig's attempt to wear down the Germans and push them 7 miles back through the mud [during the Third Battle of Ypres] had hardly been worthwhile and had been at greater expense for the Allies, who suffered 245,000 casualties compared with the Germans' 202,000.'[14]

COMRADES IN ARMS

Because of the nature of his involvement, and his commitment and resilience, especially in the fighting that took place at Pozieres, Rollo Taplin was promoted to the rank of lance corporal, effective from 15 March 1917. Two days after the end of the Battle of Bullecourt in mid-May, he was sent on leave to Great Britain. A few days later, on 22 May 1917, he received a further promotion to corporal, and in early June he rejoined his battalion. The rapidity of these promotions further underlines the extent of the battle casualties being inflicted on the AIF.

On 18 July, he was placed on the supernumerary list when he returned to Great Britain for duty with the 1st Training Battalion.[15]

It was during the second Battle of Bullecourt that future mutineer Private James Couley was awarded the Military Medal for bravery while under fire. His commendation, written by Temporary Commander Captain Alexander Mackenzie, stated:

'For conspicuous gallantry during operations 4/7 1917 as a stretcher bearer. He dressed and carried wounded under heavy enemy fire to the R.A.P. 1000 yards away. Most of these he had to carry on his back as the [s]tretcher bearers kept getting taken out. He worked for two hours without rest.'[16]

Private Couley was somewhat of an enigma, as he had previously come to the attention of his superior officers for vastly different reasons, having proven to be a significant problem for them in terms of discipline. In the 16-month period leading up to July 1917, he had committed eight disciplinary infringements that had resulted in a total of 153 days' pay being forfeited. Most of these infringements were for being AWL, but his service record does not specify why he went AWL, nor what further misdemeanours, if any, he committed while absent. Two particular offences shed some light on his behaviour. On

3 July 1916, he was charged with drunkenness while in a training camp in Etaples in France, this infringement being linked to an AWL offence. He was also found guilty of 'using improper language to a superior officer'. Perhaps the conditions that prevailed in Etaples were a factor. A common attitude among many Australians was the view that officers had to earn their respect, and did not do so just by donning stripes.[17]

Another of the few mutineers who had disciplinary charges against their names was Private Walter Martin, who re-enlisted in 1917 and was appointed to the 1st Battalion in April 1918. Martin had originally enlisted back in 1915 and had initially been appointed to the 53rd Battalion, but in March 1916 he was transferred to the 5th Pioneer Battalion. Between then and December that year, he committed numerous disciplinary offences. Finally, the military authorities decided that he had overstepped the mark and he was shipped back to Australia and discharged as 'undesirable' in March 1917.

Probably because of the government's desire to maintain a steady supply of men for the battlefront, Walter Martin was able to re-enlist just five months later, in August 1917. Once again, he was shipped overseas to England before being sent to join the 1st Battalion. It would seem that time had not mellowed his behaviour, nor his demeanour, as within the space of four months he was found guilty of being AWL on a further three occasions.

Martin and Couley had the dubious distinction of having the worst and second worst disciplinary records, respectively, of the men charged as a result of the events of 21 September 1918. Subsequently, this was to bring them to the attention of those trying to understand why the mutiny had occurred.[18]

A variety of other incidents warranted notations in the service records of those men who were later to be tried for mutiny. In November 1916, Ernest Walker was hospitalised as the result of a gunshot wound to the neck. Like Private Couley, he could be a handful for his superiors because of poor self-control, but he, too, was to later prove himself to be a man of valour. Before that, he had exhibited leadership potential, and was duly promoted to the ranks of the NCOs.[19]

Illness and disease were concerns for military authorities throughout the entire war. Under the conditions the men were forced to endure, it was very easy for diseases to spread quickly, particularly in the cramped conditions in which the men often found themselves. Dysentery and diarrhoea were particular problems stemming from unsanitary conditions, including the proximity of the men to decaying bodies. During extreme winter weather conditions, respiratory infections such as pneumonia and bronchitis were particular problems. Towards the end of the war, there were increasing numbers of influenza cases, and these were to claim more and more lives as the worldwide influenza epidemic, which ultimately claimed millions of lives, began to take hold.

One particular affliction that was a cause for concern was venereal disease. It was a matter of considerable concern to the military hierarchy that at any given time as many as 10% of trained personnel were unavailable for active duty because they were recovering from one form or another of venereal disease. The proportion of those afflicted was almost always higher among the Australian troops than among men from other nations. This can be attributed to the fact that the Australians were so far from home. Soldiers from the British army who were lucky enough to qualify for leave in Great Britain could, potentially, meet up with their loved ones. Australians were also among the war's best paid soldiers, and some of the less scrupulous British and French women were quick to take advantage of this fact. Charles Bean's brother John, a trained doctor who served in Great Britain for a time, was one officer who tried to reduce the numbers of those suffering from venereal disease.

One of his more radical suggestions was to halt the issue of condoms, as he believed that this only encouraged the men to visit brothels. His suggestion was rejected.[20]

Compared with the rest of the AIF, the incidence of venereal disease among the group of mutineers was quite low. Only 12 men in this group had suffered from the disease, and of those 12, only three had been afflicted more than once.[21]

Private Anthony Barnett was hospitalised on one occasion for venereal disease, but it was his later admissions, which occurred early in 1918, that were of the greatest personal significance for him. He suffered badly from gastritis and an abdominal ailment in the form of a ruptured appendix, which would later claim his life before he could return home to his family in Australia.[22] Private William Case spent time in hospital on at least five separate occasions suffering from, variously, rheumatism, diarrhoea, and venereal disease. However, Case, who had taken part in the original landings at Gallipoli, also spent time out of the line as the result of a string of disciplinary infringements.[23]

Conversely, Private Charles Dick, who was 28 years old when he enlisted at Henty in NSW in May 1917, had no disciplinary offences and no medical problems other than minor dental work recorded on his service record.[24] However Private Arthur Ellis, from Bathurst in NSW, was hospitalised on a number of occasions. One of those admissions related to an affliction relating to one of his heels, whilst another was the result of a gunshot wound to an ankle. At one point he was allocated to 'harvest duties', as he was deemed unfit for frontline duty.[25]

There is little doubt that, for a variety of reasons, be they disciplinary issues, medical problems or the dangers of the front line, the personal perception that each man had of his time in the army was vastly different to that he had held at the time of his enlistment.

Having been promoted twice during 1917, Rollo Taplin spent some time away from the front line due to training commitments. During the latter part of 1917, Corporal Taplin was in attendance at a gas school in Chiseldon, England. While he was there, his battalion took part in the fighting at Broodseinde (4 October 1917) and Passchendaele (26 October to 10 November 1917). He was fortunate to have been absent at this time, as these were particularly bloody battles. However, there was a considerable amount of fighting still ahead for Rollo Taplin during what were to be the final 12 months of the Great War.

One outcome from the period of time Rollo spent in training camp was his qualification as an Assistant Instructor. He then spent a short period of time at the Deverill training camp before travelling to Southampton in order to return to France, where he rejoined the 1st Infantry Battalion on 4 December 1917. Some three weeks later, he was seconded to the General Headquarters small-arms school where he spent just under three weeks before again rejoining his battalion on 14 January 1918.

A training group at the Chiseldon gas school. [photo courtesy of the Taplin family]

It would seem that Rollo Taplin spent a considerable amount of time away from the battlefront, but this situation was certainly not uncommon. Colonel Butler, the official historian for the Australian Army Medical Corps, calculated that during the 34 months between March 1916 and the end of 1918, each Australian soldier who was attached to the British Expeditionary Force (BEF) on the Western Front spent an average of just 343 days, or around 11 and a half months, on deployment to the BEF.[26] Even so, this still meant that each soldier spent, on average, about two-thirds of his time on frontline duties.

A fellow NCO whose service record closely resembled that of Rollo Taplin was Lance Corporal Ernest Besley, who was a few years older and had enlisted just before Rollo. He took part in the latter stages of the Gallipoli campaign, but they would have met up when they travelled together on board the *Ivernia* bound for Marseilles in March 1916. Both men were in D Company, and because they attended the same training schools, sometimes at the same time, it is quite probable that they became close friends.

There were some differences in terms of what fate had in store for each man or, more precisely, what each man brought upon himself. In July 1916, Besley was admitted to hospital suffering from the adverse effects of a gas-shell attack. This kept him out of action for some months. He was later hospitalised with bronchitis, another illness that impacted on his lungs. Prior to his imprisonment, Rollo had never been placed on a disciplinary charge, while Ernest Besley had gone AWL for about a fortnight whilst on leave in England in May 1918. It would seem that being on leave in England was too much of a temptation for Besley, as he was again placed on a charge, this time for disorderly behaviour, in September 1919 while awaiting his return to Australia. He and Rollo Taplin were in the same group of NCOs placed on trial on 15 October 1918, and both men were sentenced to 10 years' penal servitude.[27]

Unbeknown to them, the mutineers were now approaching what was to be the last year of the war, a year that was to prove fateful for them. They were a diverse group in terms of their ages and backgrounds. At the time of enlistment, their average age was 24 years and nine months, although 18 of them were just 18 years of age and the oldest man was 40. The vast majority of them had enlisted in 1916 or 1917, but four men enlisted as early as 1914 and a further 23 enlisted in 1915. Ninety-four of the men held the rank of private, while the remainder were NCOs. About 42% had been born in rural NSW, while 26% were from Sydney. Twenty of the mutineers had been born overseas, 18 of these being British by birth.

A key fact in relation to this group of men is that the majority of them had enlisted in 1916 or 1917, and therefore had participated in the most bitter fighting on the Western Front. Of these men, the number who had committed disciplinary infringements was fewer than those in comparable groups from other battalions. The number of were men in the group who had been rewarded for bravery was comparable to similar groups from other battalions. The difficulty in understanding why such men acted as they later did stems from the fact that any such assessment conducted now must, in the main, be based on the overall group. This is just as it was done at the field courts martial that were conducted in October 1918. The men were tried in groups of varying size. Unless specifically questioned little or no effort was made to examine the motives of the individual.

FIGHTING TO A BITTER END

As the bitter fighting continued on the Western Front during 1918, there were no indications that the war was in its final year. In fact, historians are well aware that the German military leaders took great heart from the withdrawal of Russia from the war and the spoils they gained under the Treaty of Brest-Litovsk. General Paul von Hindenburg and General Erich Ludendorff, in particular, were very keen to make whatever inroads they could against the Allies before the full impact of America's entry into the war could be felt.

The outcome of such thinking manifested itself in what is sometimes referred to as the German 'Spring Offensive'. Using troops no longer needed on the Eastern Front following the collapse of Russia, German generals began three major attacks on the Western Front. The first of these was launched late in March, and was aimed at the British Fifth Army around Arras in the Somme River area. This was followed in April by an attack centred on Lys in Flanders and in May by a third attack focusing on the Aisne area. The Germans were quite successful in their push forward, but they also became a victim of their own successes. Their gains came at the cost of very high casualty rates, as they regularly outdistanced their supply lines. By mid-June 1918, their exhausted troops were being repulsed at the Marne.

Rollo Taplin and the 1st Battalion were involved in the attack on Lys (which is sometimes referred to as the Fourth Battle of Ypres), particularly in the area around Hazebrouck, from 12 to 15 April 1918, and participated in intense fighting. Later, on 16 June 1918, Taplin was once again admitted to hospital suffering from influenza. He spent a fortnight there then spent most of the next month with the Australian Infantry

Brigade Guard, which was the platoon protecting the brigade headquarters, before returning to the front line on 28 July 1918. Once again, he was rejoining his comrades just prior to a period of intense fighting.

The stage was now set for the Allied counterattack, and the Germans were not kept waiting for long. The men of the 1st Battalion AIF were heavily involved in both the efforts to halt the German Spring Offensive and the determined counter-attack which was to follow. Their participation during the Spring Offensive centred on the fighting in the Lys area on 9 and 10 April 1918 and, in particular, Hazebrouck from 12 to 15 April 1918. The extent of the AIF's involvement during the closing stages of the war has frequently been highlighted. General Monash was later to report that from 7 March 1918 to 5 October 1918, Australian forces captured a total of 29,144 enemy soldiers and 388 guns. The ratio of the successes of the five Australian divisions to those of the rest of the British Army was 2.42, 2.40 and 2.47 in relation to the capture of prisoners, territory, and guns, respectively.[28]

The spoils of war. Piles of captured German weapons discarded after the Battle of Amiens on 8 August 1918. [AWM P01546.004]

For their part, the men of the 1st Battalion were also heavily involved in the Allied successes that occurred in the area around Amiens in August 1918. The Battle of Amiens from 8 to 11 August 1918 was the opening gambit in what was to later be known as The Hundred Days Offensive, a series of attacks that culminated in the German collapse. On the first day of this battle, Allied forces advanced 11 kilometres. This was one of the greatest advances of the entire war, and was famously described by German General Ludendorff as 'the black day of the German Army'. Fighting had again become mobile, and was to remain that way until war's end.

DOING THE WORK OF OTHERS

It is relevant to highlight one particular episode that occurred on 8 August 1918 and involved members of the 1st Battalion because it illustrates an occasion when a small group of Australian soldiers managed to achieve great results where others could not. The achievements of these men also give some credence to Monash's claims about the successes of the AIF at this time.

Charles Bean devoted more than two pages in his official history of the war to recording the exploits of two sergeants and four privates near the village of Chipilly. For him, the men exemplified the behaviour that was central to the Anzac legend. The two sergeants, 23-year-old Jack Hayes born in Hay, NSW and 21-year-old Harold Andrews, a farmer from Wauchope in NSW, had ventured into the village of Chipilly in search of souvenirs, returning with two German rifles and one machine gun. Later that same day, 8 August 1918, they were authorised to return to the village. They set off at 5.30pm, accompanied by Privates William Kane, Albert Fuller, John Turpin and George Stevens. At 6pm, Captain Berrell of the 2/10th London Regiment advised them to go no further. Ignoring his advice, they proceeded into the village. As they did so, they came under heavy fire from a ridge to the north of Chipilly.

Picture of Sergeant Harold Andrews, DCM from Wauchope in NSW. [photo courtesy of the Andrews family].

Hayes and Andrews devised a plan to outflank the Germans on the ridge, and tried to enlist the support of a British platoon, but just as the platoon arrived, British guns began to shell the area. The British withdrew, but the Australians took advantage of the heavy smoke arising from the barrage and launched an attack, quickly overrunning the first German post before moving on to a second machine-gun post. At both these posts, they captured a significant number of German prisoners and weapons.

At this stage, both British and American troops were finally arriving on the scene, but the inexperienced Americans mistook the Australians for German troops and fired at them for a brief period. In the final stanza of this action, Privates Kane and Fuller, under covering fire from their comrades, captured a further 30 prisoners. At 10pm, all six Australians returned to their unit, bringing with them one German officer, 71 men of other ranks and nine German machine guns.

As a result of this action, Sergeants Andrews and Hayes were subsequently awarded the Distinguished Conduct Medal (DCM), while Privates Kane, Fuller, Stevens and Turpin were each awarded the Military Medal.[29] Their comrades from the 1st Battalion would indeed have been proud of their achievements.

The way Australian soldiers viewed achievements such as this was seen by some as a contributing factor to the mutiny that occurred on 21 September 1918. The Australians would sometimes point out that, on occasions, Australian soldiers were capable of achieving outcomes that others were unwilling, or unable, to pursue. As a consequence, they were sometimes called upon to perform tasks that should have been allocated to others.

LARRIKIN HEROES

None of the six men involved in the event described above was involved in the mutiny of 21 September 1918. However, Sergeant Andrews was called as a witness for the prosecution when members of his own company (A Company) were tried. Moreover, the incident does relate to the background factors that led up to the mutiny. Sergeants Hayes and Andrews and their companions had certainly performed a deed that others had been reluctant to attempt. Occasions such as this had led to some resentment within the AIF over the fact that they were at times being called upon to do the work of others.

Within the group of mutineers, there were certainly men who felt that way. Also within that group were men who had received official acknowledgement of their bravery when under fire. Private James Couley had been awarded the Military Medal for carrying out his stretcher-bearer duties courageously while under fire during the second Battle of Bullecourt. Two other members of the 1st Battalion, Roger Cooney and Ernest Walker, had also been awarded the Military Medal for heroic deeds performed at about the same time, and were later gaoled as a result of the events of 21 September 1918. Like Private James Couley, both of these men had been in trouble with the military authorities on previous occasions, but both had shown that they were capable of considerable bravery when the occasion demanded. This exemplifies one of the characteristic features of the AIF that had developed by 1918. Military heroes were not always shining examples of good military discipline.

Corporal Roger Cooney was 21 years old when he enlisted in June 1915. He had been wounded in action twice, suffering a gunshot wound to the abdomen in 1916 and a further gunshot wound to his ankle in 1917. Because of this second wound, he spent most of 1917 in Britain. While there, he was found guilty of using insubordinate language to a superior officer and sentenced to 78 days' detention. This was not his first infringement. Cooney had previously been charged with desertion from the Liverpool training camp just three months after he enlisted. Later overcoming the stain of these infringements, he was able to achieve promotion to the rank of corporal, and repaid this trust by performing a deed of considerable bravery just prior to the events of 21 September 1918. Ironically, his bravery was acknowledged in the *London Gazette* of 11 December 1918 when his Military Medal award was announced. By that time, Corporal

Cooney was already in gaol, serving a sentence of eight years.[30]

The military career of Ernest Walker was remarkably similar to that of Roger Cooney. He, too, had enlisted in June 1915, at which time he had been a 25-year-old tile layer living in Sydney. He had also been wounded in the field, sustaining a gunshot wound to the neck in November 1916. This wound, plus other periods in hospital, kept him out of action for a considerable period. One difference was that after initially being attached to the 1st Battalion, he was transferred to the 61st Battalion for a short period before returning to the 1st Battalion. In August 1917, while a member of the 61st Battalion, he was sentenced to 64 days' detention for striking a superior officer. He, too, redeemed himself, and was promoted to lance corporal on 2 August 1918. His leadership skills were specifically mentioned in the citation for his Military Medal. On 23 August 1918, at Chuignes, he led his men 'in close cooperation with others and carrying them forward ... he succeeded in closing with the enemy and silencing their machine guns.' This citation appeared in the *London Gazette* of 14 May 1919, just ten days before his prison term was suspended.[31]

Not all of the larrikins among the mutineers were heroic. Some were hard men who had never adapted to army discipline. Two such examples were Privates William Case and Ernest Stokes, both of whom had been at Gallipoli. This fact alone placed both of these men within the group of 'old stagers' rather than the 'deep thinkers' who were sent to the Western Front during and after 1916. Private Case's behaviour incurred the wrath of his superiors at regular intervals, and he was placed on disciplinary charges four times during the war. Private Stokes, a 21-year-old bushman from Condobolin in NSW had enlisted at Liverpool in NSW in January 1915, and had committed a string of misdemeanours that culminated in his being sentenced to 10 years' penal servitude for drunkenness and desertion in May 1917. This sentence was quickly reduced to five years, and then in June 1917 to two years. However on 21 August 1918, having served 15 months, Stokes was released from his sentence and he returned to the 1st Battalion just one month before the mutiny occurred.[32]

By September 1918, the men entrenched on the Western Front were, as one observer noted, 'battle worn and weary'. Many had faces that were drawn and pallid, and the dull, lifeless stare of men who had endured heavy bombardments. They were so tired that many of them, when the opportunity presented, 'slept the heavy drugged sleep of utter exhaustion for twenty-four hours on end.'[33]

CHAPTER 7
THE MUTINY ON THE WESTERN FRONT

When the legends die, the dreams end; there is no more greatness.
Tecumseh (Shawnee warrior and chief)

CHAPTER 7

THE MUTINY ON THE WESTERN FRONT

When the legends die, the dreams end; there is no more greatness. Tecumseh (Shawnee warrior and chief)

THE BATTLE OF EPEHY

The men of the 1st Battalion fought in the One Hundred Days Offensive as a part of General Sir Henry Rawlinson's Fourth Army. It was under these same circumstances that they were later involved in the Battle of Epehy on 18 September 1918.

This particular battle is significant if for no other reason than the fact that it was to be the last time that the mutineers went willingly into battle before they 'walked to the rear' just three days later. In terms of military operations, it was also going to prove to be no 'walk in the park' for a number of reasons. Very few tanks were available for the attack, so instead, there would be a heavy reliance on artillery. However, in the interests of maintaining an element of surprise, there would be no preliminary bombardment. Almost 1500 guns were made available, and they would employ a creeping barrage ahead of the advancing troops. The 1st and 4th Australian Divisions were to spearhead the attack. The men of A, C and D Companies of the 1st Battalion were positioned between the villages of Hargicourt (sometimes referred to as Hesbecourt) and Villaret. They were to move forward in a northeasterly direction, while the men of B Company were held in reserve near the 1st Battalion headquarters. It was the last time that Rollo Taplin and his comrades would take part in a direct attack on the enemy.

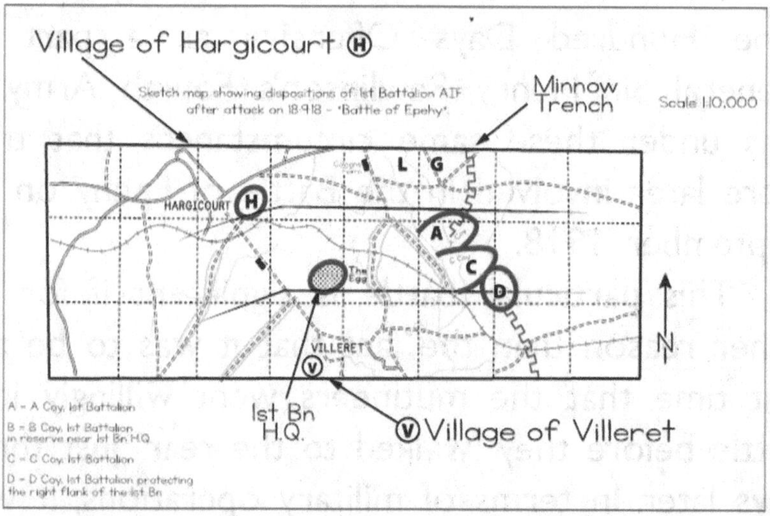

Map 1: Sketch map showing the position of the 1st Battalion AIF after their attack at Epehy on 18 September 1918.

Their progress was exceptional. With a combined strength of some 6800 men in the front line, the two divisions were able to capture 4243 prisoners, 76 guns, 300 machine guns and 30 trench mortars during the course of the day's fighting. They had advanced nearly five kilometres on a 6.4-kilometre front, and in so doing had once again achieved all of their objectives.[1]

Rollo Taplin had been in the thick of the fighting in the period from 8 to 11 August 1918, and also at Albert from 21 to 23 August 1918. His superior officers noted how well he had reacted during these battles. Upon the cessation of the fighting that took place around the town of Albert, he was given a citation for 'gallantry and devotion to duty during operations on 23/8/18.' The citation stated:

'This NCO established his Lewis gun in a position of considerable tactical value and though he exposed himself to heavy fire did excellent counter-machine-gun work, greatly assisting the advance by his prompt engagement of enemy movement.'[2]

Rollo had drawn on both his battlefield experience and the training he had received in the use of the Lewis machine gun.

We can only speculate as to what award this commendation may have elicited from the military hierarchy. What is known is the fact that the award was never made, for reasons that will soon become clear. It is possible that this may have been a 'mention in dispatches', although the degree of daring described in the citation suggests that, potentially, a higher award was under consideration.

In the closing stages of the fighting at Epehy, one of the 1st Battalion members who had made the ultimate sacrifice during the fighting was Private (SERN 3003) Allan Ernest Rostron. Private Rostron was almost the same age as Rollo Taplin and had enlisted just one month after him, and both men had arrived in France on board the *Ivernia* in March 1916. Private Rostron was carrying out messenger duties when he died. He had certainly been a courageous soldier, as he had earlier been awarded the Military Medal.

Standing: Private Allan Rostron, MM, 1st Btn AIF, killed in action during the Battle of Epehy on 18 September 1918. It is probable that Pte Rostron and Lance Corporal Taplin knew each other. Allan is standing alongside his grandfather who is believed to have been the oldest private in the AIF.
[AWM H15960]

More significant for Rollo and his comrades, and with the benefit of hindsight, was the fact that the battle of Epehy on 18 September 1918 was the precursor to the mutiny that took place just three days later.

MUTINY ON THE WESTERN FRONT

The men who were involved in the mutiny of 21st September 1918 were involved in protracted and bloody fighting during the weeks preceding that date. Of course, not all of the men were involved in all of the military achievements of the 1st Battalion. Some men had joined the battalion soon after it had left Australia, while other men were at various stages of readiness, and for various reasons, such as training or recovery from wounds, unable to go into battle with their comrades. The key point here is that the men whose actions we are about to examine were part of a military unit that was exhausted and strained beyond comprehension. From 5 April 1918 until 20 September 1918, the men of the 1st Battalion were engaged in the line for 80 days, in rear positions for 57 days and at rest or in transit for 31 days. With the constant possibility of air attacks and shelling, the conditions at the rear were very similar to those on the front line.[3]

The following summary of the events of the mutiny is based on the evidence presented in the field courts martial that followed. It also draws on Charles Bean's brief summary of the lead-up to the mutiny, as well as summaries of the trials as reviewed by other historians. In addition, it draws on the war diaries of the men of the 1st Battalion. The men were tried, mostly in small groups, in a series of field courts martial that were held as soon as possible after the event.

Having taken part in the fighting at Epehy on 18 September, the men of D Company were relieved of duty at about 8pm on 19 September and sent to the rear, which consisted of a 'sunken road' south of the village of Hargicourt, about 600 yards from the front line. Here, the men were under the command of Lieutenant George Steen. At this time, the other companies were still in deep mud nearer the front line. At about 10.30am on 20 September, the 1st Division was given a warning that they would again be called into action. This was to create some confusion, as General Sir Thomas Glasgow had decided to relieve some tired troops from the 1st Brigade. However, it was realised that there was value in using troops who were familiar with the terrain, so the decision was made to use men from the 6th Battalion to relieve the remaining men of the 1st Battalion, who would then proceed to the sunken road south of Hargicourt.

At some stage during the afternoon of 20 September, the men in the sunken road became aware that an order had been issued cancelling their rest period. The timing of this directive and just how many were made aware of the change in orders are key issues in what was to be discussed at the subsequent courts martial. What is known is that they resented this new order. Through their NCOs, the men complained to Lieutenant George Steen, saying that 'they were not getting a fair deal' and that 'they had been asked to do other people's work'. In his account, Charles Bean elaborated on this:

'There was widespread feeling that the British troops had repeatedly failed to keep up, and that the Australians, as well as fighting on their own front, were sometimes called upon to make good their neighbours' failure.'[4]

Although taken at Broodseinde Ridge, in the Ypres sector in Belgium on 12 October 1917, this picture shows terrain similar to what the 'sunken road' amy well have looked like. [AWME03864]

At about 3pm on 20 September, the NCOs told Lieutenant Steen that D Company would not take part in an attack the following day. Apparently aghast that the men were refusing to obey orders, Steen replied, 'I can't tell the Colonel this', and insisted that the orders would have to be obeyed. However, he did report the situation to the colonel because according to Lieutenant Colonel Stacy's own report, he 'had been told in the afternoon [that] the men in one company seemed very dissatisfied.'[5] Neither man took any further action and so this 'stalemate' continued past midnight. At about this time, Lieutenant Kenneth Mortlock sent for the respected Captain Hayward Moffatt to address the NCOs. Eight of them were present when he spoke to them, but it was to no avail. At about the same time, Sergeant Wood spoke to one of the NCOs, Corporal Roger Cooney, who said that all of the NCOs would join the 'hopover' (attack) but for the fact that their principles would not let them leave their men. This statement is quite significant, as a key component in the events that were about to unfold was the relationship that existed between the 'other ranks' and the men who had authority over them (the NCOs or their commanding officers). Lieutenant Steen had seemed to be concerned about the response of his commanding officer, whereas Corporal Cooney's concern was more about the reaction of the men he supervised.

Lieutenant Steen was wounded at about 3am. A Sergeant Halsthate testified that the men had stated that they had done too much, and that their nerves were gone. Sergeant Ernest Wilemett confirmed this, and went on to say that the remaining men of D Company began to move out of the sunken road in the direction of the battalion nucleus, to the rear, sometime after 3am on 21 September. He also said that he understood that their rest had been cancelled.[6]

According to Charles Bean, when the order for the attack had arrived, the men were unaware that it was to be a minor affair, nor were they specifically told that the course of action they were pursuing could be construed as mutiny, and as such, punishable by execution. When Captain Moffatt came up and told the men to join his company, all but one man refused and walked to the rear. That man, Private James Berman, was still there at 3.30am when Sergeant Wood returned to the sunken road.

Private Berman was not put on trial at the subsequent field courts martial. Born in Walcha in NSW, Private Berman had enlisted in Sydney in October 1917 at the age of 31 years and 5 months. His service record shows no record of disciplinary infringements, indeed while on leave in Britain he had courteously written to the authorities seeking permission to wed Barbara, the daughter of an English farmer. Ultimately, he and his bride returned to Australia in July 1919, but not before he had been hospitalised with jaundice. Private Berman received the order, and later opted to take part in the attack.

The attack went ahead as planned, but was relatively brief. According to Charles Bean, three companies totalling 10 officers and 84 men, including Colonel Bertie Stacy and headquarters staff, went forward. Those three companies were

A, B and C Companies. Colonel Stacy said that the members of D Company 'refused to be led except as supports', and implied that they provided this response in support of their NCOs. A relevant point to be made here is the fact that the court-martial transcripts clearly indicate that the men from D Company did not act alone; men from A, B and C Companies were also involved in the mutiny.

Colonel Stacy admitted in his report that he had not taken the men's reaction seriously, and had 'presumed that everything would be alright.' He was later informed at around midnight that the matter was serious. He wrote, quite angrily, in his report that 'the men have NOT had a hard time as we have known harder times in the past.' He had begun to seek out ringleaders, and was informed by Captain Moffatt that he had traced it back to 'one man in his company who had been a suspended sentence man.' Perhaps that man was Private James Earle.

Only one man from D Company, Private Berman, took part in this battle. The men were supported by Captain Collingwood and his men from the 2nd Battalion and Major McDonald's company from the 3rd Battalion. An ongoing German artillery barrage was the only real difficulty encountered during the actual operation. Captain Collingwood carefully moved his men through this barrage to Minnow Trench, where Colonel Stacy was situated, while the 1st Battalion held all its posts on the height. Lieutenant Colonel Stacy's headquarters did not have to be used during this attack. It achieved its objectives, but in doing so, six Australians were killed. These included Captain S. Sheen and Captain Hayward Moffatt.

In assessing the outcome of the attack, Colonel Stacy stated that 'the officers have behaved splendidly throughout but in many cases the NCOs have not realised and have sided with the men in the wrong.' He went on to say that 'I consider that the lightness and suspension of sentences in the past for desertion as greatly responsible for the trouble, and I would not care to have any of them in the Btn again if they can be transferred.' This assessment was written directly after the attack had taken place and well before the men had been placed on trial.

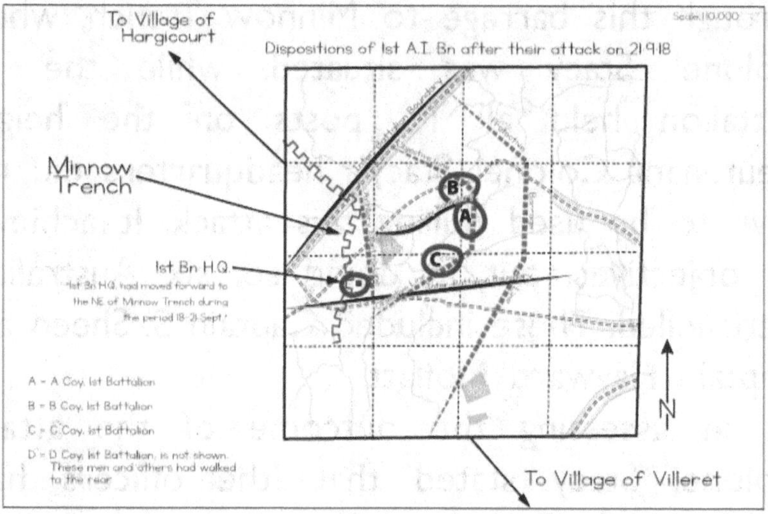

Map 2: Sketch map showing the position of the 1st Battalion AIF after their attack on 21 September 1918.

It would be reasonable to conclude that Lieutenant Colonel Stacy had already made up his mind about what had happened and why it had happened. He did, however, note that 'there was no appearance of hostility to their officers or to me in any men.'[7]

THE FIELD COURTS MARTIAL

The protest had involved men from across the entire battalion. However, the men were tried in small groups that varied in size. Five NCOs from D Company were tried together, while a further 34 men (29 privates and five NCOs) from D Company faced a separate court martial. Thirteen privates from B Company faced trial as a group, as did a further 45 men (including ten NCOs) from C Company, while 19 members of A Company, including five NCOs, were tried together. For whatever reasons, Corporal 3661 George Wethered and Lance/Sergeant 3351 Milton Hasthorpe each faced individual field courts martial. In this manner, a total of 118 men went on trial.

The first trial, which began on 15 October 1918, was of the five NCOs from D Company. These men were Corporals (SERN 3002) Albert Aylward, (SERN 3490) Rollo Charles Taplin, (SERN 3563) Roger Cooney, Temporary Corporal (SERN 4963) Henry Edward Slater and Lance Corporal (SERN 2562) Ernest Alfred Besley. They were charged with:

1. When on active service joining in a mutiny
2. Alternative charge: When on active service desertion at or about 0300 on 21/9/18 until around 0900 on 21/9/18.

The President of the Court was Major Herbert Youden (2nd Btn). Members of the Court were Captain Otto Wolff (4th Btn), Major George McDonald (3rd Btn), Captain Charles Somerset (1st Btn) and Captain Eric Johnson (HQ Aust. Corps).

This trial was significant, as it soon became apparent that the role played by the NCOs was seen to be important. It is also became apparent quite early on in the trials that the pivotal issue was going to be whether those who had 'walked to the rear' towards the battalion nucleus on the night of 20/21 September 1918 did so thinking that they had been relieved from duty, or if they did so wilfully and in defiance of warnings given to them by their officers and NCOs that there was to be an attack on the morning of 21 September.

Captain John Bootle, who had charge of the 1st Battalion's nucleus, testified that all five men were present when they were told that their relief had been cancelled. Speaking on behalf of the men, the NCOs stated that they believed they could not join the 'hopover' as, being too tired, they could not do themselves justice and also believed they would be doing a job that belonged to someone else.

In speaking for the defence, Corporal Albert Aylward stated that he heard Sergeant Ernest Wilemett say that the relief had been cancelled and that he (Aylward) believed that such a decision was not fair on the men. Earlier, Sergeant Wilemett testified that he did not recall ever saying that. Corporal Roger Cooney said, 'We were not sure if we were being attached or relieved.' When the NCOs reported the men's decision to Lieutenant Steen, Steen had replied, 'I can't tell the Colonel this.' Corporal

Cooney also testified that he thought that his fellow NCOs would 'willingly come up, only their own principles would not allow them to leave the men.' Corporal Besley tried to reason with Captain Bootle by asking him if he thought that sending the men on another attack was fair. To this, Captain Bootle replied, 'That is not for me to say.'

When called upon to make a statement, Corporal Rollo Taplin said that he had been told by Lieutenant Steen that 'in case of an attack, his platoon would be in support.' He had passed this information on to his men, and had had no trouble with them. He had then busied himself collecting containers and petrol tins. As was the case with most of the men, he had been busy doing routine tasks, and so most were not fully 'at rest'. Between midnight and 2am, he saw several groups of men moving out, and they told him they had been relieved. However, Corporal Rollo Taplin also admitted that he had received no definite orders that they had been relieved. In fact, when he heard someone call on the men to gather up their gear at 3am on 21 September, he had assumed that they were being relieved. He also questioned some of the witness statements concerning this matter.[8]

From this trial, it is clear that the defence's case rested on an apparent lack of clarity regarding a change in orders for the upcoming attack. Given that Lieutenant Steen and Sergeant Wilemett both testified that the men, or at least the NCOs, were duly warned, it would seem difficult to believe this defence. This is particularly true when that testimony is reinforced by the conversation wherein the NCOs had warned Lieutenant Steen that the men were likely to refuse to take part in the attack. However, although the orders to cancel the men's relief had been issued, it is by no means clear just how widely these orders had been conveyed.

Corporal George Wethered and Lance Sergeant Milton Hasthorpe, each of whom were tried separately, were both relatively experienced soldiers, but neither of them had lengthy experience as NCOs. Both of them expressed concern for the welfare of their men, but neither of them was certain that their men would follow if they ordered them back into the line. Hasthorpe, in fact, said that he did not stop his platoon from moving out, as he had little influence over them, stating that 'I was not the ringleader either in my Coy or in the platoon..' Both he and Wethered denied that they had been at the meeting when Captain Moffatt addressed the men.[9]

The trial of 34 members (including five NCOs) of D Company produced testimony of friction existing between some of the men and Lieutenant Kenneth Mortlock. Sergeant Wilemett testified that as the men walked out of the sunken road in the direction of the battalion nucleus at the rear, Mortlock called out that they 'were a cowardly lot of bloody swine' or words to that effect. Mortlock testified that in response, Private Couley, a Military Medal recipient, replied, 'No man calls me a coward..'

Perhaps more significant is the fact that neither Lieutenant Steen nor Sergeant Wilemett took any further action when they walked down the line and received open refusals from the men under their command. Both had the opportunity to say or do something, but neither seems to have taken that course of action.

Also significant is the fact that, among this group, the sole witness for the defendants, Private Henry Tickner, was at pains to point out that the men's complaints were about being tired and having sore feet, not about being ordered into the line again. Until they were relieved and moved back to the sunken road, they had been in a trench 'up to the knees in water and mud'. Even Colonel Stacy indicated in his report that these men would take part in the attack, but only as 'supports'.

However, not all of Tickner's evidence coincided with statements made by Colonel Stacy.

Tickner testified that the men of B Company had been doing 'ration fatigue and other fatigues'. The next day, the majority of them were part of a 'burial party, the remainder on gas guard.' Colonel Stacy was later to state his view that 'The men have NOT had a hard time, as we have known harder times in the past', but he did concede that 'the shelling has been constant near their dugouts and their nerves seemed on edge.'

Private Tickner carefully avoided any statement that might suggest that the men had met as a group to discuss their grievances. To have done so might have indicated a mutinous disposition and a premeditated plan forming among the men.[10]

It would seem that Private Tickner had good reason to be concerned about the outcome of these trials. When he had enlisted on 15 May 1916, he had been a 24-year-old married wood machinist from Sydney. He was shipped out of Australia less than three months later. In December 1916, he was admitted to hospital in England suffering from myalgia. No disciplinary infringements are recorded on his service record, but the fact that he was admitted to hospital on at least six different occasions suggests that either he was extremely unlucky or that perhaps he should never have been classified as fit for service in the first place. Between his first admission to hospital in December 1916 and his last discharge from hospital in June 1919, he suffered from pneumonia, tonsillitis and repeated attacks of scabies.[11]

The 13 privates from B Company who were tried together can be viewed as a 'mixed bag' in terms of their length of service and conduct. Most of the group had only been in France for a few months, but there were three '1915' men among them. The men's officers were only prepared to testify that the conduct of six out the 13 was 'good out of the line'. The conduct of four men was seen as 'indifferent', two were reported as being 'fair', while the remaining man's conduct was described as 'bad'.[12] One of the witnesses called by the prosecution to give evidence was Sergeant Dudley Andrews, one of the six men whose earlier gallantry, on 8 August, had already been rewarded. He had been at the battalion nucleus, and testified that he saw the accused men 'straggle in'.

It was with this group that the prosecution's case was at its strongest. This was partly due to the men's previous conduct, but also relevant was the manner in which the change in orders was conveyed. None of these men's NCOs had been prepared to walk out of the line with them.

There were only two men who were specifically charged with 'When on active service, endeavouring to persuade persons in H.M. Military Forces to join in a mutiny.' One of those men, Private James Earle, was among this group of men from B Company. As will be seen, it is relevant to briefly consider whether there were any ringleaders among the men who 'walked out of the line', and if so, who they were. Lieutenant Colonel Stacy later expressed the opinion that a contributing cause behind the entire episode was the actions of a 'few bad men'. According to the verdict reached at the courts martial, these two men were not ringleaders.

The charge against Private James Earle came as the result of a comment he made at the nucleus that had been overheard by Captain John Bootle. He is alleged to have said, 'Come on, let us get off parade...' Two of his comrades testified that he had not used those words, and so he was found 'not guilty' of the charge of persuading people to join in a mutiny.

The other man charged with inciting others to join a mutiny was Private William Case of C Company, who had enlisted in October 1914. Lieutenant Sydney Traill testified that when the men were in the sunken road, he had heard Case say, 'Come on, let us get away while the going is good...' When questioned, Lieutenant Traill conceded that he could not be entirely certain that it was Case who had said those words. As a result, Case was also found not guilty of the charge of incitement, but both he and Private Earle were found guilty of desertion.

Clear testimony was given at this trial about the manner in which the change in orders was given to the 13 privates from B Company. Lieutenant Reginald Sampson, the commander of B Company, was very definite in stating that he had clearly told the men that in the proposed attack, 'we had not far to go and did not expect much opposition.'[13]

In adopting this approach, Lieutenant Sampson seems to have been the only officer who took into account the state of exhaustion of the men under his control.

In this particular trial, only one of the accused men gave evidence for the defence. Private Arthur Mullins, a stretcher bearer who had previously been at Gallipoli, provided a four-line sworn statement in which he said that he had not been warned of the upcoming attack. As mentioned earlier, Private Mullins had committed a number of disciplinary infringements, but had also participated in the fighting. After arriving at the Western Front in company with Corporal Rollo Taplin, he had twice sustained gunshot wounds during battle. This latter fact probably made him more aware of the need to 'look out for himself', and may explain why he decided to speak up in his own defence.

However, his efforts came to naught and Private Mullins, along with all those tried with him, was sentenced to three years' penal servitude.

Other court-martial transcripts tell similar stories to those revealed in the first court martial. The men testified that they had served a significant number of hours on the front line and had been sent to the rear (the sunken road) with a promise of being relieved. The only obvious changes between each batch of transcripts seems to be minor discrepancies in terms of the exact time when a particular event occurred and the name of an officer or fellow soldier who conveyed the messages that were circulating after they left the front line. Depending on who was giving evidence, these messages were referred to either as 'orders' or as 'rumours'.

If, when reading about these 'messages/rumours', it is possible to discount the possibility of bald-faced lies and or collusion amongst the accused, it is apparent that, to say the least, there was no clear-cut chain of communication and command between the men and their superior officers. More will be said about this later.

From the outline of events presented above, it is also apparent that at no time was there a group meeting of all the men who were later charged with mutiny and desertion. Perhaps the meeting of greatest significance was that between a group of NCOs and Lieutenant Steen, which was referred to in the first court martial. The men were in smaller groups in a number of nearby locations, away from the frontline trenches. Some of them were at rest, while others were busy with designated duties such as issuing rations. This implies that there was no 'stop-work' meeting at which the influence of a 'mob' could come into play, as was the case in, for example, the Liverpool training camp riot in 1916.

That is not to say that peer pressure played no part in leading each man to the decision he made. There seems to have been a number of smaller groups that met and discussed their situation. The outcome of these discussions would then have been relayed to the others. In other words, the process by which a decision was made to 'walk out of the line' was made in a piecemeal rather than a collective manner.

Finally, there is the transcript detailing the trial of a group of 19 men from A Company.

This group included one corporal, two lance corporals and 16 privates. Many men in this group took the opportunity to speak in their own defence, and once again the emphasis was placed on confusion regarding the change in orders. Corporal William Pittock testified that neither Lieutenant Healey nor Sergeant Nichols had warned him of the attack. Similarly, Lance Corporal Sydney Carr stated that Sergeant Pritchard did not warn him of the attack. However, under cross-examination, he did concede that Pritchard had referred to a 'bit of a stunt' occurring, but was not sure whether it was official. The prosecution agreed that they had been on front-line duty from about 11am until 10pm on 20 September 1918, and were then sent to the rear.

A randomly selected service record of one of the privates reveals that this man had served continuously at Kemmel, Ypres, and in Hill 60 operations during the period from 8 August 1918 to 18 September 1918. It is of interest and relevance to note that the three NCOs were relatively young and inexperienced, and none had previously incurred a disciplinary charge. However, neither their inexperience and good service records nor the apparent confusion regarding the change in orders prevented them from receiving sentences ranging from five to eight years.[14]

A SNAPSHOT IN TIME

If an outside observer was asked to sum up, in one word, their impression of what went on in that part of the battlefront during the 24 hours or so that preceded the attack, that word would most probably be 'confusion'. In the midst of the incessant noise of artillery bombardments was a group of fatigued men who, in small groups, were either resting or performing routine tasks.

One of those tasks was the burial of bodies. As one would expect, this was always an unpleasant and distressing duty. It is quite likely that, for Corporal Rollo Taplin, this may well have been a particularly distressing occasion, coming so soon after his involvement at Epehy and assuming that he had known Private Allan Rostron personally.

Amid this sadness and confusion was a group of officers who were unsure as to how best to convey some new, unexpected and somewhat unwelcome orders. In between these groups were the NCOs, who would have been torn between their loyalty to the men beneath them and their duty to the men above them.

It is instructive to present some opinions about the men's actions that were expressed at that time. Iven Mackay, Commander of the 1st Brigade, stated his belief that the 1st Brigade was no longer what it used to be, and that 'No causes, real or imagined can ever justify such action...' Given the fact that they were in the midst of a life-and-death struggle, he is right. Mackay likened it to 'chucking a race just when there is a chance to win.' However, there were mitigating circumstances, and the fault did not entirely lie with the men who were placed on trial, nor were they manipulated by a few 'wasters', as was the view of Lieutenant Colonel Stacy, Commander of the 1st Battalion.[15]

It would be reasonable to assume that the men facing charges were well aware that assessments such as these had been made. They would also have been the subject of stares and perhaps innuendo from other soldiers, both from Australia and other countries. Some of these men would have been supportive and sympathetic, while others may have been antagonistic.

Regardless of how others felt, the mutineers themselves must have been feeling extremely apprehensive as they awaited the verdicts of their trials. What will be the outcome? How will my family and friends back home react to my being charged? How will they react if I am found guilty?

It is likely that some of the mutineers were extremely angry, but at the same time they would also have felt a sense of helplessness. Those who spoke up at the field courts martial had done all they could to explain their point of view. Their fates were now in the hands of others.

Such thoughts and fears would have been going through their minds at a time when the Great War was drawing to a close, while their comrades would simply have been thinking of when they would finally be shipped back home to Australia to be reunited with their family and friends.

THE VERDICT

Just hours later, the courts pronounced their verdicts. On the charge of 'When on active service joining in a mutiny', the men were found 'Not guilty'. On the alternative charge of 'When on active service, desertion at or about 0300 on 21/9/1918 until about 0900 on 21/9/1918', they were found 'Guilty'. Privates were sentenced to three years of penal servitude, while the NCOs were reduced to the ranks and sentenced to between five and ten years of penal servitude. These findings were later confirmed by Brigadier

General Iven Mackay, Commander of the 1st Brigade.

The key point is that a large number of men had been charged, and all had pleaded 'Not guilty' to charges of mutiny and desertion. Eleven men were found not guilty of both charges, while one was found guilty of being AWL. The remaining men were found not guilty of mutiny, but guilty of desertion.[16]

WHY 'NOT GUILTY'?

The reasons why 11 men were found not guilty of either of the two main charges are illuminating, given the fact that they were in basically the same situation as those who were found guilty. Among the 11 were two who claimed to have slept right through the attack. Given the overall level of fatigue among the group, this is quite possible. At any rate, no one was able to prove otherwise.

There were four men for whom no reasons for acquittal are on record and a signaller who claimed not to have received any orders. Another group of four men claimed to have walked away, having gained the impression that they had been relieved.

It is this group that is of interest, as their defence was basically the same as that of their comrades who were found guilty. They were found not guilty because the prosecution could find no specific evidence to say that they had been warned about the upcoming attack. This situation underlines the confusion that existed. The communication of the change in orders was not clear-cut, and this should be seen as a contributing factor to the actions taken by the men who were later charged.

Three of those who were found not guilty were members of C Company. Private Arthur Ellis was a 25-year-old train conductor when he enlisted at Bathurst in NSW in March 1916, Private Horace Clarke had been a 20-year-old labourer from Katoomba in NSW at the time of his enlistment in April 1917, and Private William Holmes had been a 21-year-old coal miner from West Maitland in NSW when he enlisted in August 1917. All three men rejoined their battalion on 26 October 1918, but none of them was to receive orders to 'go over the top' for the remainder of the hostilities.

Also of interest is the fact that the remaining man, Corporal (SERN 550) Joseph Brissett, was found not guilty of both major charges but guilty of being AWL. He claimed that he was removing a wounded man to a dressing station, even though he knew he was not meant to be doing so. Brisset was an experienced soldier, a Gallipoli veteran who had later been promoted to temporary quartermaster sergeant. Very early in the Gallipoli campaign, he had received a promotion to corporal, and at about that time had sustained a gunshot wound to the left shoulder. However, he had been absent from the front in August 1918, at which time he had threatened a military policeman. For this, he had been demoted to the rank of corporal. The court may well have been suspicious of his actions, but there was insufficient evidence for them to convict him of mutiny or desertion.[17]

The sad irony for Joseph Brissett was the fact that there had been plans to return the '1914' men to Australia earlier than other Australian troops. Had things gone as planned, he might not even have been in France on 21 September 1918.

MUTINY OR DESERTION?

There has been some debate as to why these men were found guilty of desertion rather than mutiny. The incident has invariably been referred to in this account as a mutiny because, to all intents and purposes, that is what it was. The men, or at least the vast majority of them, were not merely deserting a given position; they were ignoring a specific order. What has been brought into question, however, is the clarity with which that order was expressed.

In his thesis *A Disabling Minority: Mutiny in the First Battalion AIF, September, 1918,* John Mackenzie undertook a detailed study of this mutiny and discussed at length whether or not it was a mutiny or an act of desertion. He believed that 'the incident of 21 September 1918 satisfies the legal definition of mutiny and seems to be in keeping with the characteristics of mutinies.' The men had been reacting to a perceived grievance that they believed required attention.[18]

He gave two possible reasons why the courts martial decided to find the men guilty of desertion. The first was that they believed 'that there was some genuine confusion over the orders the men received and they were therefore not guilty of the more serious offence but were still guilty of leaving their posts without being properly relieved and were therefore guilty of deserting.' He also argued that the men were found not guilty of mutiny because this charge could have carried a death penalty, and such an outcome would have been detrimental to recruitment efforts back home. Although plausible, there is no evidence to support the view that political considerations affected the decisions of the courts martial.[19] In reality, there may well have been no time to contact the Australian government in the short period between the events of 21 September 1918 and the field courts martial.

There is another possible explanation for the verdicts the courts martial arrived at. None, or few, of the officers at that time would have failed to realise that the men had not reacted as expected on the front line. There may even have been some resentment expressed by their comrades who did go forward the next day. However, they may also have realised that these men had been through hell, and applying the full force of military law would be to ignore that reality. Being found guilty of mutiny, although technically possible but improbable, exposed those so found to the death penalty, subject to the approval of the Governor-General. This explains why so many officers gave positive evidence of the service records of the vast majority of the men, both in and out of the line.

For the former soldiers, now felons, the preceding weeks and months had been extremely stressful. They had lived on a knife's edge while their immediate futures were decided for them. Now they could only wait and see what the future would hold for them, and how their families back home would react.

CHAPTER 8
ISOLATED AND LONELY BUT NOT ALONE

Isolation is the sum total of wretchedness to a man.
Thomas Carlyle

CHAPTER 8

ISOLATED AND LONELY BUT NOT ALONE

Isolation is the sum total of wretchedness to a man.
Thomas Carlyle

After the conclusion of the field courts martial and prior to their relocation to a British prison, the guilty men were returned to their battalion to accompany it as it moved about the battlefield before later being placed in military prison compounds. During this brief period, they must have felt like they were living in a fishbowl. Collectively, they would have been concerned about how they were viewed by their former comrades. Were they pitied or were they hated? This would certainly have been the time when some of the men began to feel that they were being shunned. They had become the 'shamed Anzacs'.

The group numbered in excess of 100 men, but they were also individuals, and thus each man may have reacted in a slightly different way.

Given that a century has now passed since they were imprisoned, it is almost impossible to gauge how each man felt, and how he was regarded by his fellow soldiers. Trying to make such an assessment is even more difficult given that they were restricted in terms of communication with the outside world. Letters to home ceased.

The only support each man could look for was from the men with whom he was imprisoned, but even then there was no guarantee that such support would be forthcoming. Although they belonged to the same battalion, the men came from different companies within that battalion. They were a varied group, and so it does not necessarily follow that they were all friends in trouble together. Just as each man may have enlisted for different reasons to his comrades, so too did each man's reaction to having been found guilty of desertion differ.

Forming an opinion on why Rollo Taplin enlisted was essentially a speculative process. However, many years later, he made it very clear how he felt about the treatment he and his comrades had received. His anger was still evident some 60 years after the war ended when he was interviewed for a documentary. It would be reasonable to assume that both he and his colleagues felt a considerable degree of anger at the time.

However, these men also experienced other emotions. There were considerable degrees of confusion and bewilderment. This had been evident in some of the testimony that was given during the courts martial. There also seems to have been a view among the accused during the courts martial that 'all will be right in the end.' Individual diggers often chose not to speak in their own defence, even when they were plainly given the opportunity to do so. Rollo Taplin spoke up in his own defence on a number of occasions, but there were also times when he chose to remain silent.

This could suggest that either they trusted those in authority or that they were overwhelmed by proceedings. Perhaps there were those who did not fully realise the seriousness of the charges or who felt that it had all been a misunderstanding. In reality, they could have been found guilty of mutiny, rather than desertion, and therefore sentenced to death, subject to approval by the Governor-General.

There is little or no evidence that any of their superior officers had pointed out to them before their refusal to return to the line that they could, potentially, face the death penalty. This would have been a potent argument that could have been used to dissuade them from taking the action they chose to take. In this respect, these men had been let down by their own officers.

Again, it would be fair to assume that they were concerned about what their comrades, who were still with the battalion, thought of their actions. They would have soon gained an inkling of what these men were thinking. The guns on the Western Front fell silent about three weeks after the courts martial, but perhaps the accused men, now tried and convicted, felt the silence from their comrades well before the war ended.

It is possible that some of their comrades saw them as shirkers or cowards. However, statistics derived from their service records do not support that viewpoint. These men had experienced the horrors of the front line, some more so than others. The percentage of those among the mutineers who had been wounded was in proportion to the rest of the AIF, while the percentage who had been returned to front-line duty after having been wounded was higher than that for the rest of the AIF.[1] Eighteen of the 23 convicted NCOs had been wounded in action.[2]

The guilty men were kept in a Corps compound until 19 December, when they were transferred to No.11 Military Prison at Audricq in France. They were then shipped to Southampton, and from there, transferred to His

Majesty's Prison at Portland. For Rollo Taplin, this relocation occurred in March 1919.

It was then, and still is today, common for individuals to be concerned, in varying degrees of intensity, about what others might think of their actions. Most people like to be well thought of by their colleagues. Meanwhile, a prime concern of the military authorities was to hide this particular incident from view and get on with the war. Such episodes were not seen as conducive to military discipline and high morale. This was understandable, but such an attitude did nothing for the mental well-being of the mutineers, nor their selfesteem and personal morale.

Consequently, by and large, this incident was hidden from public view. It was never going to be good for morale, nor would it encourage others to enlist. As noted earlier, Charles Bean, who was supposedly dedicated to reporting the truth, barely mentioned the mutiny in his dispatches. A number of histories that have been written about the Great War make brief mention of the mutiny, but there are relatively few that discuss it at length. However, this is not to say that people who knew about the mutiny at the time did not have an opinion on it. Several decades later, Dale Blair recorded the recollections of one particular digger who had seen the imprisoned men whilst they were in a compound in France. This man was stunned by the sight of these men, having been told that they had walked out of the line. His view was that they had 'voted with their feet' against the situation in which they had been placed. It would seem that this particular observer was expressing some understanding of and sympathy for the men's actions; he was not condemning them.[3]

In 1979, while making the documentary *Mutiny on the Western Front,* the producers interviewed two World War I diggers and asked them for their opinions, which turned out to be divided. One felt that they had deserted their mates, while the other felt that the men had been totally exhausted and had simply followed their mates when walking out of the line. In view of the fact that this documentary graphically portrayed the horrors of the Western Front, it is likely that few modern-day viewers, as well as many from earlier generations, would see the men as cowards after viewing the horrors of the Western Front.

It is natural that the mutineers were concerned about what their families back in Australia had been told and what they were thinking. Many who had been regular letter-writers ceased writing letters. According to Rollo Taplin, they were forbidden from writing:

'You're not allowed to write home from gaol for a start. That was a penalty. None of my sisters knew. Only I couldn't tell them the facts, you see. I just made out that I had a special job to do over there and that sort of thing. Because they wouldn't let you talk.'[4]

It is likely that the 'special job' was one he invented for his family's benefit upon his ultimate return to Australia. As the war drew to a close, the first indication that many families would have had that something was amiss was when the pay that had been allotted to be sent home stopped coming. Some of the family members approached the relevant authorities, and when they eventually received a reply, it tended to be an insensitive one that revealed only partial details of what had happened. One such letter, sent as late as 18 April 1919, stated:

'In acknowledging your letter of 8th instant, I have to state that, according to the records, your brother [No.1922 Private Willie Faulkner], 1st Battalion, was sentenced on 17.10.18 to three years imprisonment for deserting His Majesty's Service. This would, no doubt, account for the stoppage of his Military Allotment.'[5]

Rollo Taplin (back row left) and three fellow soldiers from the 1st Battalion. It is not known when this picture was taken. Faces have been blurred as it is not known if these men took part in the mutiny. [photo courtesy of Taplin family]

Nowhere in this blunt, bureaucratic letter to Private Faulkner's sister was she told where he was at that particular moment. In fact, the letter was sent just before he was released. At one stage, there were 15 enquiries by family members as to why their loved ones had suddenly stopped writing. In seven of those cases, the families had only become aware that something was amiss when the pay ceased to arrive.

In one particularly sad case, Mrs Priscilla Rook had written to the army asking after her son Albert Rook. Just as the war was ending, her husband had died, leaving her with five children to support and only an allotment from her son's pay with which to support them. Eventually, in March, 1919, she received a reply similar to the one quoted above. Private Rook had been an 18-year-old hairdresser when he enlisted at Cowra in NSW on 29 January 1916. By contributing some of his pay to his family, he had shown his sense of responsibility and commitment. This was also reflected in his service record, for he had incurred no disciplinary infringements prior to the mutiny. In February 1918, he had returned to the battalion after a period of leave due to illness, only to be admitted to the Kitchener Military Hospital at Brighton in April 1918 with a gunshot wound to his left leg. He was later discharged and returned to the front line just prior to the mutiny. In many ways, he is typical of the men who were now his fellow prisoners.[6]

Potentially, the opportunity was there for those who were found guilty to not divulge what had befallen them as a result of the incident of 21 September 1918. In taking this course of action, they would have been no different from thousands of other members of the AIF who chose never to discuss the war because doing so only brought back unwanted memories of its horrors. The very fact that the 1979 documentary, despite presenting a detailed account of the mutiny and winning an award, was apparently only able to locate and interview a single participant speaks volumes about reluctant people were to talk about it.

The suggestion that the men kept the matter to themselves would seem to be supported by a letter written in 1968 by one of their number who had fought at Gallipoli. He sent in an application for his Gallipoli medal so that he could 'give it to my grandsons, as they are always asking me about the landing and I would very much like them to have it.'[7] This man, Private Alan Barclay, had arrived in France on board the *Ivernia* alongside Rollo Taplin, and, like Rollo, had apparently decided not to tell his family about his involvement in the events of 21 September 1918.

Very little is known about what became of the mutineers in their post-war lives. There is anecdotal evidence that only one of the convicted men ever joined the 1st Battalion Association after the war ended.

One of the accused, about whom considerable post-war details are known, is Rollo Taplin, who died in 1981, just two years after he provided the anonymous voice-over for the documentary *Mutiny on the Western Front*. His anonymity disappeared, at least for members of his immediate family, when they recognised his voice and questioned him about the interview, at which point he admitted that he was the anonymous digger. He had asked the makers of the documentary to keep his name a secret, not so much because of the shame he felt, despite the passage of 60 years, but because he said that if his identity was revealed, 'he would have no way of disciplining his grandchildren if they knew he had rejected discipline in action.'[8] At that time, his eldest grandchild was still a teenager.

In 1979, Rollo Taplin's attitude was quite obviously one of anger at the lack of what he deemed would have been a more appropriate course of action by the relevant military authorities as the incident unfolded. In the documentary, he angrily stated:

'Look, Stacy's (Commanding Officer, 1st Battalion) job was to be there, quick and lively, and say, "Look men, I know you're tired. Just be patient." No they don't say that because he's the hierarchy and we're just skunks ... Well I got ten years ... We were really hostile for the injustice. Not the punishment, the injustice of the whole affair ... My son has never forgotten or forgiven me for not taking him in to an Anzac march. He doesn't know why and I'm not going to tell him. No one else is going to tell him.'[9]

Corporal Rollo Taplin had no doubt that with better, more proactive leadership from the commanding officers the men would have reacted differently.

In March 1919, Rollo Taplin disembarked at Southampton on his way to His Majesty's Prison at Portland, where he was to complete his sentence, although on Anzac Day in 1919, his sentence was suspended. On 6 July, he boarded the *Boorara* for the trip back to Australia, arriving on 26 August 1919. At about that time, his war medals, the 1914/15 Star, the British War Medal and the Victory Medal, were returned to him. Nothing came of his previous commendation for a bravery award.

Initially, the military authorities decided that the men would not receive their campaign medals. This decision was later rescinded, and the medals were presented to the men, but some were only received as late as 1922. At no stage was there any suggestion that bravery awards that had previously been bestowed on some of the mutineers were to be rescinded. There are also records in some of the soldiers' files noting that they were considered eligible for repatriation benefits.[10]

When the decision was made to try these men for desertion and mutiny, the trials were held soon after, and verdicts were quickly reached. The same haste was definitely not evident when the decision was made to release the men and return them to Australia. This is not a comment on the nature of the field courts martial, but has more to do with the difficulty of shipping a large number of men back home. The first sentence suspensions occurred, ironically, on Anzac Day in 1919, some sentences were suspended on 24 May 1919, more were suspended on 18 June 1919, and one was suspended on 14 September 1919. It is possible, even probable, that those men who were the last to be released had less likelihood of successfully concealing their imprisonment from their families. In July 1919, the Australian government granted amnesties to all AIF soldiers in military prisons and detention centres and remitted their sentences.[11]

Amid this bureaucratic decision-making there are a number of poignant, even sad stories. There is one particularly poignant story that perhaps gives an indication of the shame felt by these men. Private Anthony Barnett, a 19-year-old Sydney printer when he enlisted, had gone AWL during the period after his court martial and before entering prison. For this offence, he received an extension of his sentence and was not released until January 1920, but he again absented himself in South Africa whilst homeward bound before reporting in sick, suffering from acute appendicitis. His condition subsequently deteriorated and he died from peritonitis on 1 June 1920. After enlisting in August 1916, this particular soldier had not presented a disciplinary problem, and apart from one bout of venereal disease, had experienced no medical problems. There is no obvious indication as to why he seemed reluctant to return to Australia. Maybe his sense of shame was the reason.[12]

Private Barnett was not the only prisoner who did not make it back to his loved ones in Australia. Private Charles Johnstone, who had been a 21-year-old box maker in Sydney at the time of his enlistment in September 1917, died in a military hospital in Calais on 16 January 1919. At some stage prior to his death he made out his will, in which he bequeathed his worldly goods to his mother Louisa Johnstone of Gladesville in NSW. His service record states that he died of 'chronic interactional nephritis' and he was buried in Les Baraques Military Cemetery just west of Calais. Charles Johnstone would never know that many years later, in September 1961, a public-spirited citizen would find a service medal near Moorabbin in Victoria that was inscribed with Private Johnstone's name and number. Presumably this medal had been a part of his bequest to his mother. It was duly posted to the Army Medal Section at Victoria Barracks in Melbourne.[13]

Equally sad but much more perplexing was the situation of Private Richard Stafford (also known as Charles Riddett), who died of influenza, also in Calais, on 19 March 1919, just two months after Charles Johnstone. Stafford was a Roman Catholic, and at the time of his enlistment on 5 July 1917 he had named his father, Stanley Dickson, as his next of kin. On 15 November 1917, he wrote his will in which he bequeathed all of his possessions to his mother, Sophie Riddett. Given his use of two different names and the fact that his parents had different surnames, Richard Stafford would certainly have posed a series of questions for anyone researching his family tree.

He had been a 22-year-old labourer from Wollongong when he enlisted, and his early medical record stated that he had never been vaccinated and had no dental issues, but did have a deformed toe on his left foot. He did not join up with the 1st Battalion until May 1918, and two months later was allocated to 'harvesting work'. He rejoined the battalion on 19 August 1918. Just over two years after the mutiny, his mother asked if she could be sent some pictures of his grave in the cemetery at Calais. She was told that two pictures could be supplied at a cost of threepence each.[14]

Neither Stafford nor Johnstone had any disciplinary infringements recorded against their names prior to the mutiny, and neither man made it out of France; they both died before they could be sent to prison in England.

Apparently, not all of the men who had been tried for mutiny and imprisoned for desertion thought ill of the army. At least one man, Private Gordon Loughrey, re-enlisted during the Second World War. He had been an 18-year-old civil servant in Sydney when he first enlisted in July 1917.

WHAT HISTORY HAS HAD TO SAY

The official response to the mutiny by the military authorities was delivered in the court-martial verdicts. However it was not long before others expressed their opinions in writing as to why the men had acted as they had. In reviewing some of these responses, the focus will be on the discussion that centred on why the men did what they did.

The commanding officer of the 1st Battalion, Lieutenant Colonel Bertie Stacy, was one of the first to express an opinion. The official Australian war historian, Charles Bean, had not been in the immediate area at the time of the mutiny, and had made only a brief mention of it, but he did put forward his view on why it had occurred. It has also been pointed out that Bean was quite keen to provide material that supported the Anzac legend, so it reasonable to assume that he was not going to dwell on material that contradicted that legend.

A survey of what has been written about the mutiny of 21 September 1918 in the almost 100 years since it occurred has been a revelation. Many histories do not mention it at all, and quite a few mention it almost in passing, and then only briefly. A large percentage of these histories, when they express an opinion on its causes, do so along the lines offered by Bean. Only a handful of writers have discussed the mutiny at length, and of those discussions that could be found, only one focused solely on it. This was John Mackenzie's unpublished BA Honours thesis. Three other studies discussed the mutiny and its causes at some length, but in those cases the discussion was part of a broader topic; they were not studying this mutiny in isolation. Complicating the matter even further is the fact that of these four 'extensive' studies, two have not been published.

This is not to say that serious, well-known historians have ignored the mutiny of 21 September 1918. There are many who know it well, understand what caused it and have an opinion on it. However, they have chosen not to write about it in depth. When they have written about it, it has usually been in the context of other, broader issues, such battle fatigue, shell-shock, or military discipline.

Some historians have mentioned it as part of a study of military mutinies in general and how this particular mutiny relates to other mutinies. Other historians have examined how the different nations dealt with the mutinies with which they were confronted during the Great

War and why some nations were more likely than others to experience rebelliousness in the ranks.

The period during which Bean's views, and those similar to his, were prevalent was quite lengthy. This may be a generalisation, and there were no doubt exceptions, but it would seem that this was the case for several decades.

Then, in 1979, came the award-winning documentary *Mutiny on the Western Front*. The potential impact of film in helping to form opinions is enormous, and can only increase. As the pace at which we live our lives increases, people will be much more likely to view a film than to read a book about an event, let alone consult source material. It is likely that this documentary unleashed an interest in, or at least an increased knowledge of, the mutiny of 21 September 1918. The four studies, two published and two unpublished, that discuss this particular mutiny, either in isolation or as part of a larger study, were all written in the years following the screening of *Mutiny on the Western Front*.

When John Mackenzie, a BA Honours student, wrote his thesis on the mutiny he was a student at the Australian Defence Force Academy. Potentially he brought a 'military' perspective to his study. In the years since then, a number of other historians have written about this mutiny at some length. The following chapter presents a survey of some of the views that have been expressed regarding the mutiny of 21 September 1918.

This historiographical survey focuses on the 'why' behind the mutiny. There is no assumption that the survey is conclusive; no doubt the opinions of some will have been overlooked. However, the survey is quite extensive, and so each viewpoint has been summarised as concisely as possible. Comparisons between viewpoints are also provided. All of these opinions are well-informed and make for interesting reading. Naturally, this author also has an opinion on what happened, which has already been partly revealed, and will be clarified later.

CHAPTER 9
NOR THE YEARS CONDEMN...

History will be kind to me for I intend to write it.
Winston Churchill

CHAPTER 9

NOR THE YEARS CONDEMN...

History will be kind to me for I intend to write it.
Winston Churchill

Charles Bean preceded his discussion of this mutiny by placing it within the context of other issues and events occurring at that time. He noted that during 1918, General Monash had actively promoted the achievements of the AIF in the field. Monash had complained to General Headquarters that the British press was not giving full credit to the Australians for their achievements. In addition, he circulated extracts from the British and French presses among the Australian troops highlighting their achievements. Bean believed that Monash was deliberately trying to get more from his men by appealing to their aura of prestige, rather than their patriotism.[1]

Prime Minister Billy Hughes was also seeking more publicity for the Australians' achievements, but for a different reason. After touring the battlefield near Amiens during 1918, he declared that the Australians were a 'decisive factor', and if that belief was to become more widely known, it might increase Australia's bargaining power at any future peace settlement.[2]

Having elaborated on the Australians' achievements during August 1918, Bean went on to discuss the mutiny that had occurred in the 59th Battalion in early September 1918. This mutiny had also been a refusal mutiny, and was briefly discussed in an earlier chapter. These two refusal mutinies had a lot in common. In both instances, the men were being ordered back into the line while resting after a sustained period of fighting. On both occasions, the men felt they were being asked to do the work of others.

Charles Bean also discussed the disbandment mutinies. It is within this background that Bean briefly gives his view on the mutiny of 21 September 1918 and his reasons for the actions taken by the men. Bean said that the men had clearly made their feelings known to Lieutenant Steen when they had said that 'they were not getting a fair deal'. In summary, Bean's view was that 'the British troops had failed to keep up, and that the Australians, as well as fighting on their own front, were sometimes called on to make good their neighbour's failure.'[3] Bean was well aware, and did concede, that the British, especially the Fourth British Army, were also suffering, but he felt that the Australians were continuing to be called on because of the successes they had achieved.

It seems to be the case that Charles Bean was keen to continue to promote the Digger/Anzac legend image of the Australian soldier, even if doing so came at the expense of the British troops. This situation certainly explains why he expended less ink writing about this refusal mutiny than he did writing about, for example, the exploits of Sergeants Andrews and Hayes and their men on 8 August 1918. Over the years, Australian readers have been receptive to views such as these. This also helps explain why Australians often forget that ours were not the only troops who fought at Gallipoli.

Charles Bean would have been well aware of the views on the 21 September refusal mutiny expressed by the commanding officer of the 1st Battalion, Lieutenant Colonel Bertie Stacy. Bean was not in the immediate vicinity at the time of the mutiny, and so much of the little that he did write about it came from other sources, including official reports.

Colonel Stacy formed the conclusion that the protest was largely the result of 'over-mention of the troops in the newspapers, so that they over-valued themselves in comparison with others.' Stacy also believed that there were 'bad soldiers' among the group who were able to influence how the group would react. This view, which seems to say that the men were the victims of a few 'bad eggs', is one of the earliest opinions offered on the cause of their actions. However, the field courts martial failed to substantiate the view that a few bad eggs had been the cause. Those men charged with inciting the mutiny had been found not guilty. However, Stacy also saw the role of the NCOs as pivotal, stating his belief that 'in many cases NCOs ... have sided with the men in the wrong.'[4]

Charles Bean seems to agree with Colonel Stacy on the influence of 'bad men' when he says that 'in contrast to the mutiny of the 1st Battalion, it [a disbandment mutiny] had its origins in some of the best men and the finest qualities of the AIF....' Yet it could also be concluded that he was talking more about the nature of the disbandment mutiny than the quality of the men involved. The mutiny in the 1st Battalion was in a totally different category to the disbandment mutinies because of why it occurred.

For several decades, little was said about the events of 21 September 1918, and the incident was pushed into the background. Generally speaking, the men returning from the battlefront were focussed on a return to a normal life, as were the communities to which they were returning. For most observers, it was more palatable to promote the Anzac legend, the view that Australian troops were indispensable. The men may already have been shunned by their comrades, and now they found that their view of the circumstances had been ignored, and so most of them chose to remain silent. When the mutiny was discussed and its causes reviewed, it was done so in terms of ill-disciplined men with perceived rather than real grievances given that many men from other battalions had suffered through the same horrific conditions these men had endured. Thus, the views aired by Colonel Stacy and seemingly endorsed by Charles Bean tended to hold sway.

Six decades after the war's end came the *Mutiny on the Western Front* documentary. Much of this documentary was devoted to underlining the horrific conditions that existed on the battlefields of the Western Front. The mud, the blood and the noise were all graphically illustrated with stark footage. There was extensive discussion of how the men had reacted, and reference was made to the 'lucky ones' who had received a 'blighty' ... a wound that would require treatment back in Britain. Views on courage and the training and circumstances that fostered it were also discussed.

There was extensive discussion of the mutiny itself. Two First World War diggers were interviewed about their war experiences and, when asked about the mutiny, they both understood why it had occurred, but had differing views on whether or not the men were justified in reacting in the way they had. In addition, as stated earlier, there was also the angry and anonymous airing of an opinion by a man we now know to be Corporal Rollo Taplin.

It is not too far-fetched to suggest that this documentary was a watershed. The events of the mutiny were now out in the open, and more people became aware of it. It was only going to be a matter of time before a closer, more detailed study was made of the circumstances and some assessment made regarding its causes.

MORE RECENT OPINIONS

In 1988, John Mackenzie made a detailed analysis of the mutiny of 21 September 1918. He was studying this mutiny in isolation in an attempt to define it and analyse why it had occurred. By this time, most, if not all of the mutineers would have passed on, and yet Mackenzie felt that it was still a sensitive topic and so when referring to specific individuals to illustrate his points, he gave each of them a *nom de guerre*, using the names of some of his fellow students.

He began by examining the episode in the context of what had happened in the lead-up period. In the 12 months or so prior to the mutiny, there was a significant increase in desertions (and AWL charges, which were sometimes actually desertions). The 1st Battalion was particularly affected.

In examining the reasons for the mutiny occurring among this particular group of men, Mackenzie initially focused on the two premises that had already been put forward. These were that the men had been overworked, and that the group was influenced by a few illdisciplined men.

First, he examined the workload of the men of the 1st Battalion. In the period leading up to 17 September, he concluded that there was nothing to suggest that these men were subjected to a greater workload than the men of other units. However, the men of the 1st Battalion suffered the most in the period from 18 to 22 September, which includes the date of the mutiny. In other words, there is some evidence to support the view that these men were being asked to do more than others. Thus, Mackenzie felt that this explained why the mutiny occurred at this particular time, but it didn't fully explain why it occurred amongst this particular group of men.

FIRST BRIGADE CASUALTIES 18-22 SEPTEMBER

Battalion	Officers	Other Ranks
1st Battalion	13	108
2nd Battalion	4	73
3rd Battalion	6	91
4th Battalion	2	62

The above graph gives support to the view that during the days preceding 21 September 1918, the men of the 1st Battalion were subjected to a heavier workload. The casualty rate among the officers of the 1st Battalion was double that of any other battalion in the 1st Brigade.][5]

Hence, Mackenzie also saw the need to investigate the character and background of the men. Bean had suggested that this was a relevant factor, and Stacy saw it as a key factor. To do this, he examined their records, in particular their length of service, medical records, any commendations they had received and their disciplinary records. Mackenzie also examined their previous occupations, religious denomination and marital status. He concluded that 'the mutineers show no extraordinary pattern of offences or common features that suggest that they were any different to those men who did not mutiny.'[6]

In surveying the occupational backgrounds of the men involved, Mackenzie was determining whether or not it was an industrial-style worker's dispute wherein men from certain occupations, especially unskilled occupations, were more likely to mutiny than others. He found that the cross-section of occupations among the men who mutinied was similar to that of men from other battalions who did not mutiny. He therefore dismissed occupation as a relevant factor. Similarly, Mackenzie surveyed the religious background of both the men who mutinied and those who did not. The vast majority of the men who mutinied were Church of England, with just 25.8% being Roman Catholic. Believing that the latter group were more likely to question British authority, Mackenzie concluded that religious affiliation did not appear to have influenced their decision to walk out of the line.

More importantly, he came to the conclusion that it was more pertinent to examine the men's behaviour since joining the AIF than to look at the scant available information about their former lives, such as employment and marital status. He began by looking at the time these men had spent in battle, using it to gauge the extent of battle fatigue that they must have been suffering. He drew on studies of combat effectiveness based on World War II (but seen as also relevant to World War I) that pointed out 'that the most accepted figure for the length of time required to reach combat effectiveness is ninety days.' Conversely, men could become 'mentally unbalanced by the fear of death' after a period of six months.[7] Mackenzie examined the dates of enlistment of all the 'mutineers', as well as the dates when they joined their units. From this he concluded that:

'The figures ... suggest that the men involved in the mutiny are perfect candidates for being ineffective. Those who had not yet experienced ninety days of combat were not yet effective soldiers and those who had been involved for longer periods were subject to "war weariness" or "battle fatigue".'

In short, the mutiny should be viewed in terms of the resilience built up and retained by the men rather than their disciplinary records or former occupations.[8]

However, it is highly likely that, once again, these men were no different from their comrades, so Mackenzie went on to examine other potential reasons for their refusal. Although a large number of the men had been soldiers for some time, they had not, for various reasons, spent a lot of time recently with their unit or in combat. Sixty-two of the mutineers had returned to the unit from hospital, while a further three had returned from leave following a period of hospitalisation and two had returned from specialist training schools to which they had been sent after completing a period of convalescence. Further analysis of these statistics revealed that 58 men had been wounded in action (13 of them more than once), whilst 77 had been removed at various times after falling ill. Some had suffered illnesses as many as four times, but the number who had contracted VD was surprisingly small.[9]

Army records indicated that four of the mutineers had previously suffered from shell-shock, but all of these cases had occurred in 1916, and there was no further mention of this particular problem. However, that does not necessarily mean that this problem did not exist for some men; it simply means that it was not recorded as such.

From this, Mackenzie concluded that 'the mutiny is unlikely to have been the result of physiological problems as there are no indications of recurring physical or mental problems...'[10] While this may have been the case, it is relevant to note that significant mental-health issues may have been present for at least some of the men who mutinied, but they would not have been taken into account either because they went unrecognised or they were deliberately concealed. Mackenzie makes a valid point when he states that 'The number of men who returned from sickness and wounds can reasonably be expected to have made them more fearful of being wounded again.'[11]

The point being made here is that, whilst overall morale was seen to be good, it was at the personal level that problems were more likely to arise. For that reason, and also because the matter was raised by Colonel Stacy, Mackenzie then examined the disciplinary records of the mutineers.

When talking about the mutineers, Colonel Stacy had this to say:

'I have not been able of course yet to discover the ringleaders, but Captain Moffatt informed me he had traced it all to one man in his Company who was a suspended sentence man and I think the same will be found in the other Companies, namely men with bad records have induced the others to leave and others had been too weak not to follow.'[12] Two men, Private James Earle and Private William Case, had been charged with inciting others to mutiny, but both men had been found not guilty due to lack of supporting evidence.

In fact, the vast majority of the men had few or no disciplinary charges in their service records. However, there were some repeat offenders, including two men who had ten and 12 charges, respectively. One of these men, Private James Couley, had been awarded the Military Medal in July 1917. He was one of three mutineers to whom this award had been made. The other, Private Walter Martin, who had 12 disciplinary offences on his record, had previously been sent home and discharged before rejoining the unit in April 1918 and subsequently committing his final three disciplinary infringements. Mackenzie concluded that neither of these men had been in a position to have influenced others in making the decision to walk out of the line.[13][14]

Nor is Stacy's conclusion about bad men inciting others to mutiny sustained by the courts martial. Regarding the two men charged with inciting others to mutiny, Private Earle had no previous charges, while Private Case had only four charges over a four-year period. Neither of the two worst disciplinary cases appears to have been a ringleader, nor were those accused of having taken leading roles, Earle and Case, found guilty of incitement.

FIRST BATTALION MUTINEER'S CONDUCT RECORDS

Infringements	Count
0	72
1	26
2	10
3	8
4	3
5	1
6	4
10	1
12	1

This graph shows that 78% of the mutineers had incurred either no disciplinary infringements or just one infringement.

An examination of Private James Earle's service record shows that he was extremely unlikely to ever become a rebellious ringleader. It not only shows that he had no disciplinary infringements, but also shows that, during the war, he met and married Ethel Barwell of Peckham in England. In September 1923, he lost his 'R.S. badge' when some of his clothes were stolen. At about that time, he applied to base records for 'any medals and emblems due to him'. He was subsequently sent the 1914/1915 Star, the War Service Medal and the Victory Medal.[15]

Private Case was somewhat different. A Gallipoli veteran, he had been found guilty of disciplinary charges on four occasions, but also suffered from a variety of health problems. Aside from being hospitalised for venereal disease, he had been admitted for rheumatism on several occasions and for lumbago and scabies at least twice. Apparently, he is the 'suspended sentence man' to whom Colonel Stacy had referred, and yet he must have had some pride in his war service, for on 18 April 1966 he applied for his Gallipoli medallion.[16]

Thus, it would appear that Stacy was wrong when he concluded that the men had been led into mutiny by a few 'bad soldiers'. Mackenzie concluded that the men who mutinied were representative of the entire AIF.

An examination of the court-martial transcripts shows that time and time again the officers who gave evidence testified that the general behaviour of the men, both in and out of the line, was good. For example, Captain Charles Somerset testified that he had known 31 of the men and found them to be 'men of excellent character both in and out of the line ... the [eight] NCOs named have always shown keenness, and have proved reliable men.'[17]

Mackenzie thus seriously questioned two of the reasons put forward to explain the actions of the men of the 1st Battalion. The first was that these men had been overworked. While the men had been subjected to considerable stress, they had been no more overworked than other units of the AIF. He did, however, identify as a relevant factor the fact that many of the men were at a stage where their battle effectiveness was reduced because of the time they had spent in battle and because they had recently been out of the line for one reason or another. 'Given their lengths of time in combat these men were in stages of "combat effectiveness" that makes them candidates for breakdown.'[18]

Mackenzie concluded that they mutinied because of general dissatisfaction exacerbated by a particular grievance (the change in their orders). They were influenced by a general democratic spirit that existed among the Australian troops, as evidenced by the earlier refusal mutiny. In fact, even Stacy had mentioned that as a factor. Mackenzie also stated his belief that given the conditions that prevailed on the battlefields of the Western Front, it was somewhat surprising that more combat refusals had not occurred within the AIF.[19]

There is little doubt that Mackenzie has made an extremely worthwhile contribution to an outsider's understanding of this particular mutiny. His was the first study to comprehensively survey the group of gaoled men in an effort to establish their motivation. As he was a student at the Australian Defence Force Academy, his unpublished study was undertaken from the perspective of an historian with a military background. Others who later wrote about this mutiny read Mackenzie's study and made reference to it in supporting their viewpoints.

THE ANZAC LEGEND

In 1997, Dale Blair also analysed the nature and causes of this particular mutiny, but unlike Mackenzie, he was not focusing on the mutiny itself. His book *Dinkum Diggers: An Australian Battalion at War* set out to examine the Anzac legend so often talked about on Anzac Day and as presented by Charles Bean. To do this, he closely examined the wartime experience of the 1st Battalion and came to the view that they had, at times, an overly positive view of their own abilities that was not always matched by their performance. Only 'the prominence of the Australians in the pursuit of final victory in 1918 provides a compelling conclusion to the often average performances to that time.'[20]

Blair echoed Mackenzie's view that the incident on 21 September 1918 was clearly a case of mutiny, even though the men were found guilty of desertion. He went on to examine the reasons behind the men's actions, and began by restating their belief that their actions were justified, as they were being overworked. For him, the trigger for the mutiny was 'the cancellation of a planned relief on the night of 20 September and the rumour that the battalion was to participate in another attack the following morning.'[21] While battle fatigue was certainly 'a major contributing factor ... it cannot be advanced as the sole reason for the outbreak of the mutiny.'[22]

Blair, too, examined the men's service records, in particular their time spent in battle and their time away from the front line as a result of being hospitalised, and came to the conclusion that these men were somewhat short on experience and that because of losses incurred during a war of attrition, the battalion's cohesion had been weakened. As a result, it was hard for them to maintain an *esprit de corps* sufficient to withstand the 'discomforts, dangers and dissatisfaction that are so much a part of war.'[23]

Summary of Absentees and Rejoiners reported during the period from June 1 to August 3 1918. (Absentees: those absent for more than seven days.)[24]

	British		Australian	
	Absent	Rejoined	Absent	Rejoined
June 8, 1918	134	127	118	94
June 15, 1918	135	161	104	136
June 22, 1918	94	107	104	118
June 29, 1918	104	151	97	98
July 6, 1918	108	112	60	86
July 13, 1918	116	175	82	79
July 20, 1918	80	91	114	58
July 27, 1918	173	138	134	128
August 3, 1918	118	106	121	101
Totals	**1,062**	**1,168**	**934**	**898**

As the statistics show, the situation whereby individual allied soldiers were away from their battalion for extensive periods had been in existence for some considerable time prior to September 1918. These absences could be for a variety of reasons, such as normal leave, sick leave (including for treatment of venereal diseases), recovery from wounds (including self-inflicted and accidental wounds) and training programs. Between March 1916 and the end of 1918, some 306,243 men of the AIF were deployed in France, but there was a total 'wastage' (absence of men) of 199,812 men from all causes.[25]

Blair disagreed with the view held by Australian officers, such as Lieutenant Traill, that the absence of the death penalty encouraged the men to react in the way they did, and instead saw the social background of the men as a possible factor. Blair pointed out that 62.89% of the mutineers were from occupations designated 'tradesman', 'labourer' or 'industrial and manufacturing', whereas for non-mutineers this figure was 43.99%. The statistics comparing the former occupations of the mutineers with those of non-mutineers from the 1st Battalion are largely similar for the two groups, apart from four categories. There were slightly more professional and clerical workers among the non-mutineers, whilst there were 15.21% more labourers among the mutineers; and 25.80% of the mutineers were Catholics, as opposed to 14.66% of the non-mutineers. Based on this, he suggests that 'the higher number of men from blue-collar occupations and Catholics, who were highly represented in this category ... were more receptive to demonstrating their grievances than those from white-collar backgrounds.'[26]

In other words, he was examining the potential role and outlook of men who were

Catholic and also unskilled workers. He felt that there did not seem to be any solid basis for any argument suggesting that previous occupation and religious denomination were significant factors in causing the actions taken by the mutineers. They were, however, factors that may have made them more likely to take action leading to a refusal.

In his study, Blair took a close look at the relationship between the mutineers and their leaders (both NCOs and officers). During the courts martial, the officers had testified to the previous good conduct of the mutineers, but in the period leading up to the refusal, their own leadership had not been as effective as it could have been. Added to this was the loss of some officers just prior to the attack (Lieutenants George Steen and Wesley Blake were both wounded). However, even before then, their leadership had been ineffective. It was Lieutenant Steen who had said, 'I can't tell the Colonel this.' Blair recorded that Lieutenant Blake had previously been described by fellow officer Lieutenant Richards as a 'little self-important man ... [who] could do nothing better or higher in this world than talk about himself.'[27]

In between these officers and the men were the NCOs, and it was with regard to this group that Dale Blair expressed the opinion that they 'were the most cruelly served'. Some of them were inexperienced. For example, Albert Aylward had only been a corporal for four months. They were torn between obedience to their superiors and loyalty to their own men, for whom they would have felt responsible. To make matters worse, they felt obliged to act as spokesmen for the men. When the sentences were handed down, they received terms ranging from five to ten years as opposed to the three-year terms given to the men.[28]

Blair also examined the challenges presented by the task of reassimilating men who were returning to the battalion after leave. Even Captain Moffatt, widely acclaimed as an effective leader, had been unable to successfully reason with the men. Thus, Blair concluded that 'ultimately ... it was a lack of communication, trust and intimacy in the officer–man relationship that was responsible for the final breakdown of discipline.'[29]

This conclusion is one with which this author fully agrees, and it will be further elaborated on at the conclusion of this historiographical survey. Dale Blair's book is definitely thought-provoking, and his contribution to the discussion on the mutiny of 21 September 1918, although not a lengthy one, is well founded. In making a study of the Digger image as portrayed by the Anzac legend, Blair was questioning the accuracy of some of the myths that have formed. In doing so, he provided a starting point from which to better understand the mutiny of 21 September 1918.

SOME 21st-CENTURY OPINIONS

In 2009, Edward Garstang wrote an unpublished PhD thesis on the topic of crime and punishment on the Western Front and provided extensive commentary on this particular refusal mutiny as part of a larger study of British army discipline. His account of the various courts martial, in particular, is detailed and thorough, and his bibliography indicates that he had read the studies of both John Mackenzie and Dale Blair.

Garstang also believed that at least part of the blame for the mutiny could be attributed to the army hierarchy because of the confusion they created regarding the proposed relief. He pointed out that of all the commanding officers, only one, Lieutenant Reginald Sampson, told the men that the planned 'hopover' was to be a minor affair. He also saw some basis in the argument that fatigue played a crucial role, as the men had been heavily involved since early August, and two days before the mutiny occurred, even Colonel Stacy had written in his diary that the men were 'not up to concert pitch'.[30]

Like Mackenzie, he noted that for a variety of reasons there had recently been a rapid turnover of men within the battalion. This had impacted upon unit cohesion and, paradoxically in his view, the men came together 'not in battle but in refusing to fight.' Like Dale Blair, he also took a closer look at the relationship between the NCOs and the men, as well as that between the NCOs and their superiors, and pointed out that the NCOs were relatively inexperienced, and yet they 'exerted a greater degree of control over their men than did the officers in charge of the individual platoons.'[31]

Finally, Garstang explored the issue of whether this mutiny should be viewed as an industrial matter. He made detailed reference to Mackenzie's statistics on the occupational and religious affiliations of the men and concluded that 'the convicted men saw their actions as industrial rather than mutinous.' None of their officers had warned them that they could, in fact, face a firing squad. In the absence of the death penalty and with the example of the Peronne mutiny of 5 September, for which no one was punished, before them, they must have felt that they could escape the full weight of the law. In this, Garstang concluded, they were wrong.[32]

Garstang is not the only historian to have taken the view that the action of the men in walking out of the line was industrial action. Both Mackenzie and Blair had also investigated this particular viewpoint. There is no doubt that the men saw themselves as having continually being asked to do the work of others, but the fact of the matter is that these men were in a military, rather than an industrial situation.

In such a situation, obedience is crucial. The men must have realised that they would have to face the consequences of their actions; they just didn't realise that facing a charge of mutiny and potentially a firing squad would be amongst those consequences. However, Garstang did clearly point out the possibility that the mutineers may well have believed that they would not face serious charges because of what had happened following the refusal mutiny that had occurred just over two weeks earlier.

Another historian who has made a study of this mutiny is Ashley Ekins, whose special areas of interest are the Vietnam War and World War I. In particular, he has looked at stress and fatigue among front-line soldiers. In 2010, he outlined his views in an article titled 'Fighting to Exhaustion: Morale, Discipline and Combat Effectiveness in the Armies of 1918' that appeared in a book titled *1918 Year of Victory:*

The End of the Great War and the Shaping of History, which he edited.

Ekins believes that Charles Bean's assessment that the mutiny was caused by a few 'bad characters' was based on his romantic assessment of the AIF and Colonel Stacy's conclusion. Stacy was a strict disciplinarian who saw multiple factors at play, and was disgusted with the leniency of the sentences handed down to the mutineers. Previously, he had tried to identify the ringleaders. Ekins concluded that 'The 1st Battalion contained a few "hard cases" but no more than any other AIF unit and these men do not appear to have influenced the mutineers significantly.'[33] Like other historians, he saw that the men were motivated by an interplay of several factors:

'Other factors which played a greater part were overlooked, both by senior commanders and Bean in his official history. Soldiers were suffering from general operational fatigue, exacerbated by lack of sleep and exposure to enemy fire under difficult conditions. Men were carrying out ration fatigues under heavy shellfire and in holding trenches filled with water and mud up to their knees for two days before the attack.'[34]

Many historians, in writing about this mutiny, had seen it as an episode brought on by fatigue, but not all of them expressed it as succinctly as that. Ekins, too, stated that whilst the 1st Battalion had been involved in heavy fighting during the previous month, their exposure had been no greater than that of other battalions. In saying this, he was echoing an opinion presented by John Mackenzie. He believed that the refusal resulted from a particular grievance; the men had been promised relief, and by going on the attack they would not be getting a fair deal, as they would then be doing someone else's work. Dale Blair also saw this change in orders as the trigger for the mutiny.[35]

Because he was looking at this particular mutiny as part of a broader study of exhaustion and morale, Ekins also examined other types of mutinies within the AIF, as well as how various motivating factors came into play within different national armies. His was an extensive study, and he drew a number of interesting conclusions. Agreeing that 'refusal' mutinies were the most serious type of mutiny, he concluded that 'the more intriguing question is not why the mutinies occurred, but why there were so few and why some armies remained immune.'[36] Once again, in saying this, he was echoing views expressed by other historians such as John Mackenzie.

It was in relation to this question that Ekins provided an extremely interesting point of view.

He felt that the 'efficiency and impartiality of systems of military justice might account for some variations between national armies', but also relevant was 'the comparative social composition of national armies.' The French, Italian and Russian armies were 'predominantly composed of peasants, whereas the British army largely came from a disciplined industrial labour force.' This meant that the British soldier was more likely to obey his officers as a result of a sense of 'social deference among the British working class civilians from which the soldiers were drawn.'[37]

In saying this, Ekins was echoing the views of Lord Moran, the decorated doctor from the British Army Medical Corps who had experienced the Great War. Lord Moran had noted that social compositions and outlooks differed among various national armies. However, Ekins also pointed out that in accepting this point of view, care should be taken not to downplay obvious factors such as leadership, comradeship and unit cohesion.[38]

In briefly discussing this particular mutiny, Peter Stanley began by referring to the background situation and the 'trigger' that set it off. The men were suffering from exhaustion, and they were angry because their relief had been cancelled. He also raised points that had been mentioned by other historians. Among the group, there were only about a dozen '1914–1915' men, and of the remainder a large number had only recently returned to the unit after absences for reasons such as hospitalisation. Such absences could be expected to make each man more apprehensive about his situation.

A key point for Stanley is his view that the 'resolutely civilian character' of the men led them to protest about having to do other people's work and 'not getting a fair deal'.[39] This implies that the men saw the mutiny as an industrial matter. They also felt they would get away with their protest because of the light sentences that had been handed down for recent instances of AWL and desertion.

Stanley was scathing in his assessment of the manner in which certain officers had misread and mishandled the entire affair. Colonel Bertie Stacy's belief that the mutiny was the work of a few ringleaders was inaccurate. Lieutenant Sydney Traill thought his fellow officers erred in trying to ingratiate themselves with the men rather than taking a firm hand. Only the Brigade Commander, Iven Mackay, while not condoning the men's actions, had realised that there had been a change in their 'spirit, energy and discipline'.[40]

Writing in 2014, Nathan Wise also took the view that the actions of the men stemmed from their view of 'military service as a job of work'. In refusing to attack, the men's response was 'another piece of industrial action'. Like others before him, he referred to the men's claims that they were overworked. He quoted Blair's analysis of their occupational background as being 'a factor in the decision to mutiny'. Also relevant was the fact that the AIF was a volunteer army.[41]

Nathan Wise did make the valid point that a protest such as that which occurred on 21 September 1918 would not have occurred earlier in the war. At Gallipoli, and again in 1916 and 1917, the 'devastating casualties suffered by the Australians contributed towards a sense of fatalism.' It was only in 1918, when successes led to a greater sense of self-assurance, that the men felt they could make a protest without fear of reprisal.[42]

In the documentary *Mutiny on the Western Front*, British historian John Terraine expressed the view that this particular mutiny was the result of the men's exhaustion. There is no doubt that this was a key factor, but it was not the only factor. What has become apparent is that recent historical analysis has turned away from those assessments made just after the mutiny occurred. For example, the role played by a few 'bad eggs' is no longer seen as valid. However, as will be shown, not all of the potential causes that were put forward quite early on should be dismissed.

It remains to underline various opinions, already briefly outlined, as to why the men took such drastic action, and whether or not they are deserving of a greater sense of understanding, even sympathy, rather than the shame that most of them were forced to suffer in silence.

CHAPTER 10
WITH THE BENEFIT OF HINDSIGHT

When it is obvious that the goals cannot be reached, don't adjust the goals; adjust the action steps.
Confucius

CHAPTER 10

WITH THE BENEFIT OF HINDSIGHT

When it is obvious that the goals cannot be reached, don't adjust the goals; adjust the action steps.
Confucius

Having examined the events that took place near Hargicourt on the Western Front on 20 and 21 September 1918 and having placed them within the context of the background and experiences of the men involved and army disciplinary procedures, what conclusions can be drawn? It has become clear that this mutiny did not stem from the actions of a few ill-disciplined men.

Broadly summarising the opinions that have emerged during the past three or four decades, several common features appear. Although found guilty of desertion, the men were actually guilty of mutiny, as they had walked out of the line. Fatigue has been widely seen as a significant background factor, and the spark that ignited their protest was the unexpected change in orders that denied them respite from front-line duties. Also relevant was the time that many members of the 1st Battalion had spent away from their unit. However, in both of these aspects, fatigue and time away from the unit, the men of the 1st Battalion were in a similar situation to that of their comrades in other battalions. Nor was this group of men markedly different from other groups, both in their own and other battalions, in terms of previous occupation and religious denomination. The mutiny did not derive from the actions of a small group of men with a poor disciplinary record; in fact, there were few such men within the group.

Many observers also felt that the NCOs had been placed in a difficult situation and, as a result of their actions, were harshly treated. There is no doubt that the punishments the NCOs received were significantly harsher than those meted out to the privates. Finally, there has been some consensus that given the conditions that prevailed on the Western Front, it is somewhat surprising that there weren't more refusal mutinies. The number of such mutinies in the AIF was small, as was the number of men involved. Other countries, such as France, had to deal with larger-scale mutinies that had a much greater impact on their battle effectiveness.

Analysis of the motives behind this mutiny has been a difficult task at many levels. It has been difficult to identify those men who were found guilty and imprisoned, as opposed to those who were found not guilty, and it is probable that they would have preferred that it had stayed that way. The court-martial proceedings were not widely available to the general public until relatively recently. At the time of the mutiny, even the families of the mutineers remained uninformed. The mutineers themselves would have had neither the means nor the motivation to write a personal diary of the proceedings and their imprisonment. Consequently, the only version of events that was available was contained in the official summary accounts of the field courts martial. All of this has since changed.

Another difficulty lies in the still-developing field involving an understanding of trauma stemming from war. Some progress was made during the Great War, but there was still a long way to go. Shellshock had become an accepted term at official levels, and there was some understanding of its causes rather than a dismissal of it as being due to 'weak character'. For example, before the war's end, incessant artillery bombardment was recognised as a major factor that could result in observable physical symptoms. However, since the end of that war, our understanding of mental trauma has developed a lot further. Compare the attention given to returning Vietnam veterans with today's knowledge of post-traumatic stress and projects such as Soldier On, which specifically focuses on those who have returned from war with significant disabilities. Prince Harry, for one, spends a considerable amount of his time and energy working for and with such veterans, and has established the Invictus Games, an international sporting event for disabled veterans.

In discussing this mutiny, there has been only passing reference made to the disbandment mutinies that also occurred in September 1918. This was intentional, because these mutinies were never treated as mutinies, and no charges were laid. The men maintained a form of military discipline and, for the most part, had the support of their officers, either openly or covertly.

The only similar mutiny about which any significant information is available is that involving the men of the 59th Battalion that took place at Peronne just prior to 21 September 1918. However, there are some minor differences between this earlier mutiny and the one under discussion here. A larger number of men were involved in the mutiny discussed here, and the men who mutinied at Peronne had been ordered to attack, whereas the men of the 1st Battalion had had their original orders (that they were to be relieved) reversed. The refusal by the 59th Battalion was short-lived. The authorities took little or no action, and although some men were found guilty, their sentences were later remitted.

Yet the mutiny at Peronne should be seen as significant in terms of its impact on the mutiny within the 1st Battalion. It is highly likely that the latter group had heard about the Peronne mutiny and the way in which it had been resolved, as well as the outcome for the men involved. In addition, there is no evidence indicating that the men of the 1st Battalion were told about the possibly extremely serious consequences of their actions. They may have been aware that the death penalty was an unlikely, but possible outcome, but there is little or no evidence to support the view that they were told this by their officers, or so it would seem.

Relative to the progress of the war, it is also relevant to note that there would have been a markedly different set of circumstances in play between when the men mutinied and when they appeared before a series of field courts martial some two to three weeks later. On 21 September 1918, none of the men walking out of the line could have been aware that this was to be their battalion's last action. Most, if not all, of them and their comrades in other areas of the front line would not have known that the war was within weeks of its conclusion.

However, by the time of the courts martial, circumstances had altered somewhat. Many members of the AIF would have known, or at least assumed, that they were no longer going to be called into battle. In fact, the first court martial on 15 October was held some ten days after the last occasion on which any Australian soldiers had been involved in military action on the Western Front (see Appendix 8). This situation may explain why so many officers gave positive reports of the conduct of the men on trial, both in and out of the line. Even men who had been repeat offenders, such as the Military Medal recipient James Couley, were given satisfactory reports.

Were the men who were gaoled guilty of mutiny? Definitely. The episode of 21 September 1918 has been referred to as a mutiny even though none of the men were found guilty of this offence. This is because they committed the offence of mutiny, even though that was not the offence for which they were found guilty. Both John Mackenzie and Dale Blair explored this matter in depth. There is no doubt that by taking the action they did, the men were disobeying an order, which was an act of mutiny. What is in doubt is the manner in which that order was conveyed.

This was examined in depth during the courts martial, and is deserving of further examination, but there is also another question to pose.

Did the men who walked out of the line do the wrong thing? In terms of letting down their comrades and in terms of disobedience in response to military orders ... yes, it is reasonable to conclude that they did the wrong thing.

But not everything in life is clear-cut, or black-and-white; there were mitigating circumstances. Some of these, such as exhaustion and being overworked, related to most members of the AIF and other national armies who were in the area at that time. There were also other special circumstances that related to this group of men in particular. Once these are taken into account, it is reasonable to conclude that they were harshly treated and were not deserving of the shame with which they were ultimately burdened. These men were in a state of extreme fatigue, but so too were many men in other units who did not react in the same way. Many of these men came from a social background that rendered them more likely to protest than others who came from a more privileged background, but this also applied to other men from nearby units who did not protest. So what was different?

Part of the answer lies in the make-up of the group that was ultimately gaoled. There were some experienced campaigners among the group, but there was also a significant percentage who had, in recent months, spent time away from their unit in a hospital or at training schools. Even some of the NCOs were new to their role and did not know their men well. Cohesion was not as tight as it might have been.

Perhaps more significant than this is the fact that most of the group had reached that stage of battle experience where they could not be considered inexperienced, but could no longer be viewed as effective. This was pointed out by both Mackenzie and Blair. It is likely that few observers at that time would have been aware of this, although both Colonel Stacy and Major General Glasgow had both noted a decline in commitment and morale. It is likely that a similar situation may have applied to some of the men in other units. Approximately half of the group had, at some stage, been wounded, some of them more than once. These men would have felt a heightened sense of anxiety and apprehension. This must also be seen as relevant to the decision they made.

There seems to be a discernible difference between the circumstances that existed at the time of the incident and those in play at the field courts martial. Initially, the men may not have realised that their actions would be seen as a mutiny. Apparently, none of their officers warned them of this possibility. It is likely that they later came to realise that they were in a more serious situation than they had initially thought. The men may have believed they would be punished for going AWL or, at worst, desertion. By the time the courts martial commenced, they were seeing things differently. That may explain why, to some observers such as Garstang, the men were at pains to avoid giving the impression that they had met as a group, or in small groups, to discuss what action they should adopt in relation to their grievances. To have done so would have suggested a premeditated plan of refusal. However, it must also be pointed out that if all the mutineers had gathered as a group at some point, it would have been then that they would have received a clear direction that they were to return to the front line.

Their grievances centred squarely on the fact that having been heavily committed in battle for an extensive period during the fighting at Epehy and having been told they were being relieved, they were now being told that they were once again to take part in a 'hopover'. This change of plans came while heavy shelling was going on about them and some of the men were still performing tasks such as burial duty.

A number of historians have likened their reaction to that of industrial action. There is no doubt that the men were making a protest in response to what they perceived as an intolerable situation, and so, yes, it is reasonable to see this as an industrial grievance.

However, not every observer would see it that way. The men were not in a workplace; they were in a military group that was on a battlefield. It was a life-or-death situation. The army is a hierarchy, not a democracy. Never, at any stage, were their superiors going to agree that they had the right to lodge such a protest. Nathan Wise's point, that such a protest would have been unlikely earlier in the war, is a valid one. Then, as in 1918, survival was vital, but by September 1918 there had been signs that Allied military successes were lasting rather than temporary.

The men may have erred, but the mutiny could well have been prevented, and some of the mutineers were dealt with unnecessarily harshly.

This point has particular relevance, as Dale Blair pointed out, to the group of NCOs. They were 'caught between a rock and a hard place'. On the one hand, they would have seen it as their duty to pass on and obey orders, but on the other hand they were well aware of the plight of their men, having shared the same battlefront conditions. Some historians point to their leadership inexperience as a factor leading to the response they provided.

There is an alternative viewpoint. Those who were new to their responsibilities in supervising a small group of men may well have seen their prime function as caring for the welfare of those men. If the men were being dealt a harsh blow, then it was their role to speak up for them. This they tried to do, but to no avail.

However, there is no evidence to suggest that they then directed their men to walk out of the line. Some of the men had already come to that decision. Hence, there must be other mitigating factors that led to this situation. There were certainly circumstances in play that help to explain why this particular group of men took the action they did. One factor, the lack of clear communication of the change in orders, is made clear in the court-martial transcripts. Another, the issue of leadership, is briefly mentioned by both John Mackenzie and Dale Blair. It was also clearly and unequivocally cited by Corporal Rollo

Taplin when he angrily referred to Colonel Stacy's response.

The mutineers had been exposed to front-line conditions over an extended period of time and, individually, they were at differing stages in terms of being candidates for battle fatigue. However they were not atypical in this respect. Fatigued? Yes. Stressed? Yes. But no more so than men in other units who were alongside them and to whom the same expectations applied.

So ... what other light can be shed on why these particular men chose to take the action they did?

The answer lies in the particular circumstances surrounding this incident and the leadership that was provided at the time. The lines of communication that were in operation at that time also warrant investigation.

EFFECTIVE LEADERSHIP

Effective leaders are decisive. They weigh up the pros and cons of any situation prior to making a decision, but they do not procrastinate. They make the best decision based on the available information; they don't make a particular decision because they know that it will be the most popular among their men.

A good leader also communicates well with his men, giving clear, concise instructions that are neither vague nor confusing. When this broad area of leadership is examined carefully in terms of the actual instructions given to the men, it allows the actions of the mutineers to be better understood. The actions taken by the mutineers can be placed into a better context, one that sets them apart, even if only marginally, from their comrades.

In elaborating on this opinion, it must be made clear that there is no intention to denigrate the military careers of the officers involved. By and large, these men were capable soldiers with proven records. To a large extent, circumstances were against them; everything was happening quite quickly, there was incessant artillery bombardment and most of the events were played out under cover of darkness. The following delineation of events is a juxtaposition and should be seen as sequential ('A' happened, then 'B' happened) rather than causal ('A' caused 'B' to happen).

Even the account of the incident provided in the *History of the First Battalion, AIF, 1914–1919* indicates that things were happening quickly; there were a few unknowns and some confusion. It states, in part, that 'The ground was quite unknown to us, as was the approach to the jumping off place, and there was little time for reconnaissance.' Again ... 'The companies were given a warning order to prepare, but did not receive their definite orders until later. The men became disgruntled at the news that they were not going out on relief ... but until night came it was not realised that the men would take any serious action.'[1]

The NCOs were the group that was most in tune with what the mutineers had been through and their state of mind. News of the proposed attack, reaching some of the men as a rumour, caused them some alarm. They approached the company commander, Lieutenant George Steen, to discuss the matter and the reply they received was a dismissive, 'I can't tell the Colonel this'.[2] In the ensuing bombardment, Lieutenant Steen was himself wounded at about 2.30am on 21 September 1918, along with Lieutenant Wesley Blake, but according to Dale Blair both men were wounded well after Steen had been approached by the NCOs. Blair concluded that Steen 'had ample time to alert his commanding officer to the developing crisis but chose to do so only when the situation had further deteriorated.'[3]

After Steen had been wounded, Lieutenant Kenneth Mortlock took command of D Company and sent for the highly respected Captain

Hayward Moffatt to address the men. Moffatt told the NCOs that it was their duty to get the men involved.[4] This approach, whilst potentially more effective than Steen's response, 'failed to move the men.'[5] Captain John Bootle's response to a question put to him by one of the NCOs was 'It's not for me to say.' This is probably not the type of reply needed at a time when these men were seeking guidance.

The attack went ahead, successfully and with relatively minor losses, but sadly Captain Moffatt was among the fatalities.

The point being made here is that at a time of crisis, the men to whom the NCOs would normally defer (their immediate superiors) either responded ineffectively or responded when it was really too late to be effective. As quoted above, the response by at least one, if not two, of the officers was almost akin to Pontius Pilate washing his hands of the whole affair. By the time Captain Moffatt was called in to persuade the men, it was too late for him to have any impact, regardless of what he said.

Further allegations of questionable leadership qualities among some of the junior officers were made during the courts martial. Lieutenant Sydney Traill believed that the prosecution's case had been weakened because many officers had attested to the good characters of the soldiers being charged. He believed that they did this because 'they were frightened of not making themselves good fellows with the men. A common fault with officers these days.'[6]

For purposes of comparison, it is useful to revisit the response by another Australian officer when faced with a similar set of circumstances. The officer concerned is Brigadier General Harold 'Pompey' Elliott.

Pompey Elliott was an experienced soldier who had won a DCM for bravery during the Boer War. One historian, whilst talking about his role during the infamous battle of Fromelles in 1916, described him as 'instantly recognised as a soldier's soldier; a man with the ability to lead by example, sometimes a little too instinctively, but at the same time a man with the capacity to speak as an equal with his men.'[7]

Studio portrait of Brigadier General H.E. 'Pompey' Elliott, CB, CMG, DSO, BA, LLM. Elliott has been widely seen as one of Australia's most effective and popular leaders of the First World War. [AWM A03084]

Elliott successfully resolved a disbandment mutiny involving his men that occurred late in September 1918, just after the mutiny discussed here. More relevant to the present discussion was his involvement with the earlier combat refusal involving members of the 59th Battalion that occurred near Peronne on 5 September 1918. This particular mutiny had a lot in common with the mutiny involving the men of the 1st Battalion.

The men involved in the Peronne mutiny were also looking forward to a break when they were once again ordered to pursue retreating Germans. About 60 men refused to take part, as they were suffering exhaustion and felt they were being overworked. Upon hearing of their actions, Pompey Elliott sent one of his officers to ask the men to write out a statement of their grievances. The main grievances listed were exhaustion, overwork, lack of relief and the fact that the Australian command had not actively brought their plight to the attention of their British superiors.

Elliott, who was known for his explosive outbursts, went to the men and spoke to them calmly but persuasively. He stated that he had read their grievances and agreed that they had cause for complaint, but that they were going about it in the wrong way. What they were doing amounted to a serious crime, and was a slur on the battalion and their gallant comrades. He went on to point out that in a previous mutiny in 1797 involving men of the British navy, the mutineers had also had genuine grievances, but the ringleaders were shot nonetheless. Finally, he told the men that he would adjourn while they considered what he had said. If, when he returned, they were still determined to go ahead with their actions, he would send them to the rear but he would also speak on their behalf when the matter was later officially investigated. Elliott's response had been most effective; when he returned, the men indicated that they would rejoin the battalion.

In asking the men to write down their grievances, he had given them time to think things over (and cool down). He had made it clear to them what their duty was, but at the same time he had shown that he understood their plight. Furthermore, he was true to his word. Elliott later followed up on some of the specific grievances listed by the men, conducting investigations into the amount of food they were receiving and the care provided by the medical officer.

'Elliott's response to this challenging situation confirmed the quality of his leadership.'[8] What he did not do was wash his hands of the matter and allow the men's grievances to fester and worsen.

Comparisons can be odious, but in some ways Pompey Elliott exhibited leadership attributes that were not shown by others. There were other times when his actions and attitude incurred the wrath of his superiors, but showing a concern for his men's welfare was a key issue for him. One biographer told of how he had been able to get the men in his unit to salute officers automatically, while failure to do so was a recurrent problem in other units. Elliott had explained to his men that saluting smartly was a sign of the discipline needed to make them better fighters.[9] This is not to say that Pompey Elliott did not also employ threats to gain obedience, even if they were threats he knew he had little chance of carrying out. On one occasion, he bellowed that he would have any man who was caught looting shot. On another, he threatened the same fate for any man who passed on false rumours about advances made by the Germans.[10] In taking this approach, he was in company with many other Australian military leaders, including Monash.

Corporal Rollo Taplin, one of the NCOs involved, would have welcomed such a response. Some 61 years later, he clearly underlined the differences between proactive and ineffective leadership responses when he remarked:

'Look, Stacy's job was to be there, quick and lively, and say, "Look men, I know you're tired, just be patient." No. They don't say that, because he's the hierarchy and we're only skunks.'[11]

Bertie Stacy was known as a strict disciplinarian, and as such, may have been unpopular with some of his men. The entry for him in the *Australian Dictionary of Biography* notes that 'his austerity and dogged determination to see a task through had sometimes made him unpopular.'[12] However, he had also been seen as an effective leader, as evidenced by the commendation for a Bar to his DSO that was written one month prior to the mutiny. This commendation praised his reconnaissance and organisational skills prior to and during an attack on Chuignolles and Chuignes on 23 August 1918. It would seem that Colonel Stacy chose not to get involved, even though he knew that something was amiss as early as the afternoon of the day before the attack. In fairness, it should be noted that Stacy may not have been fully informed of the seriousness of the matter until it was too late to act effectively.

Similarly, Lieutenant Steen's leadership effectiveness may have been compromised by his level of fatigue and the incessant artillery bombardment leading up to his wounding. For his part, Lieutenant Blake was a recent addition to this unit, and so would have been less familiar with the mood of the men he was leading.

GOOD COMMUNICATION

In discussing the relevance of effective communication, there is an apocryphal anecdote, seemingly more jocular than factual, that illustrates how important it is for instructions to be clear and concise. In this anecdote, an officer at the front line relays the following message back to his superiors in the rear trenches:

'Send reinforcements. We're going to advance.'

However, because the message is relayed verbally, the message that arrives at headquarters is:

'Send three and fourpence. We're going to a dance.'

The anecdote may be frivolous, but its message is relevant. Instructions must be given in a direct and unambiguous manner so that there can be no misunderstanding.

In terms of the refusal mutiny of 21st September 1918, the focal point of confusion for the men was the issuing and then subsequent cancellation of the order that they were to be relieved of front-line duties. It was not that the orders had been misheard; it was more a case of confusion as to which orders were relevant. Extensive reading of the court-martial transcripts reveals some anomalies as to when the men were informed that their period of rest had been cancelled and they were now being directed to ready themselves for a 'hopover' that was soon to take place. At their trials, many of the mutineers had given the defence that they believed they had been relieved. The most succinct way to summarise this situation is to quickly revisit what John Mackenzie discovered about the group of 11 men who were charged but were found not guilty.

Of these 11 men, there were two who claimed to have slept through the attack, 'four men who claimed to have gone out under the impression that they were relieved, a signaller who claimed not to have received any orders, four men who have no reasons (for acquittal) indicated ... and one Non-commissioned Officer (Corporal Brisset) who took a wounded man to a dressing station and on his return found the 1st Battalion had gone.' As Mackenzie points out, the four men who claimed they had been relieved were acquitted because 'the prosecution was unable to show that they had been specifically warned of the attack.' Brisset was found not guilty of mutiny for the same reason, but was found guilty of being AWL.[13]

The key point here is that if the testimony of these men is to be believed, it provides evidence of the fact that some confusion existed relative to the issuing and later cancellation of the order that they were to be relieved. Clarity of communication is an essential element of good leadership.

Before leaving this point about leadership, consideration should be given to the leadership role of the NCOs who were found guilty of desertion. As stated earlier, these men were in an invidious situation. As the men's immediate leaders, they were well aware of the mood and physical condition of the men in their charge. They would also have seen themselves as having responsibility for the welfare of their men. Colonel Stacy indicated how he saw the role they played in the mutiny, and it is tempting to conclude that perhaps, in his mind, they became the 'bad eggs' that the courts martial failed to identify. However, he did not state this, in fact he wrote that the NCOs had not been abusive when approaching him, although some of them may not have realised that siding with the men was wrong.

They ultimately accompanied their men in walking out of the line, but there is no evidence that they led this response, even if they were willing participants. 'When the penalties were handed down by the court, the NCOs were dealt with in the harshest manner; most received terms of five to ten years' imprisonment as opposed to the three years handed down to the other ranks.'[14]

It is ironic that they incurred heavier penalties because of how they saw their position as leaders when they themselves had been let down by ineffective leadership.

Regardless of the rights or wrongs of the actions of the men who were subsequently imprisoned, it is probable that without the tumult and confusion that existed at that time, the men may have reacted differently. Had there been clearer communication of orders at the time when it was needed and more proactive and effective leadership, it is highly likely that the mutiny would not have occurred. These are the factors that best underline the difference between this particular group of men and other members of the AIF. The men who were imprisoned were not deserving of the shame with which they were burdened. Despite their grievances and in view of the needs of their comrades, they may well have joined them in the attack.

We will never know.

CHAPTER 11
LIFE GOES ON...

*We're all islands shouting
lies to each other across seas
of misunderstanding.*
Rudyard Kipling

CHAPTER 11

LIFE GOES ON...

We're all islands shouting lies to each other across seas of misunderstanding. Rudyard Kipling

NOT NAMED BUT SHAMED

When first considering researching and writing about the courts martial arising from the events of 21 September 1918, I described the situation to a returned serviceman who had fought in the Vietnam War. His immediate reaction was, 'That topic is best left buried.' The inevitable assumption behind that comment seems to be that he had concluded that the men had behaved dishonourably; perhaps he saw them as cowards.

However, proper historical analysis does not work that way. There is always another side to any story, more evidence to be uncovered. Debate still continues over the significance of the 1854 Eureka Stockade rebellion on the Ballarat goldfields. Was it Australia's first real push for democracy, or were the gold-diggers merely protesting about the oppressive licence-fee system? The list of such questions is endless.

One observer of mutinies in general has stated some views that resonate strongly with reference to this mutiny. Tom Wintringham noted that 'there is a strange lack of books on mutinies', but that it 'seems probable that one reason for history's reticence is the difficulty in passing judgement on those who took part in these events.'

'Mutinies—revolts by men under discipline of life and death, do not happen lightly, and in most cases when reasons for the mutiny are sought, they appear to be ... conditions of life that few of us would find tolerable. The puzzle becomes, not why did the mutiny occur, but why did men, for years or generations, endure the torments against which, in the end they revolted.'[1]

It is ironic that the men of the 1st Battalion have been shamed because they took part in a mutiny when in fact they were found guilty of desertion. It is generally agreed that their actions were, in fact, mutinous, and it is true that their sentences were longer than those handed down to most others found guilty of desertion, especially those of the NCOs. However, the fact remains that as deserters, they were not a rarity within the AIF. Poor discipline among the Australians has been noted by many historians. Edward Garstang stated that 'as an approximate guide ... one in fourteen Australians, one in fifty New Zealanders and one in twenty Canadians faced a court martial.'[2] During 1917, the AIF experienced a rate of desertion approximately four times that of any other Dominion force.[3]

An examination of the service records of all of the men who were charged reveals that their disciplinary records were as good as, if not better than, other members of the AIF. More than half of these men had no disciplinary infringements at all, and those with no more than two infringements constituted 85% of the group. Individually and as a group, they had played their part. About half of them had been wounded, some more than once. The percentage of men who had suffered from venereal disease was no higher, indeed probably lower than that among other groups within the AIF.

As mentioned earlier, two former First World War diggers were interviewed some 60 years later about their views on the mutiny, and their opinions were divided. One of them fully understood the actions of those gaoled, particularly in view of what they had been through, while the other was less forgiving, saying that you should never let your mates down. This diversity is probably a fair reflection of the varying attitudes among the general population today.

For those who do not know the military records of the mutineers and the background circumstances prior to the mutiny, the prevailing attitude is most likely to be one of condemnation. Regardless of the individual personalities within the group of mutineers and their personal war service records, the group has generally been treated as a single entity. They have been 'tarred with the same brush'.

For several decades, the events of 21 September 1918 were seldom spoken about and even less frequently written about. At worst, the men, both individually and as a group, were ostracised. At the time of writing *Dinkum Diggers: An Australian Battalion at War* in 1997, Dale Blair was able to report that of all the men charged with mutiny, only one name appeared on the membership list of the 1st Battalion Association. He also stated that apart from Rollo Taplin's then anonymous comment, none of the men had left a record of their involvement.[4] Those men who were able to avoid being shunned by the wider community probably only did so because those around them did not know of their involvement. For 60 years, Rollo Taplin's family did not know that he had been involved. The fact remains that the experiences and behaviour of these men remain part of the overall story of the AIF during the Great War.

However, once greater knowledge of their actions has been attained, there will most likely be a greater understanding, a greater sense of empathy. Dale Blair canvassed viewers of the 1979 documentary *Mutiny on the Western Front*. He believed that this documentary had taken a sympathetic view that had 'struck a chord with the show's audience.' He went on to say that one viewer stated that the mutineers could never be seen as cowards or criminals. Instead, they were 'quiet heroes'.[5]

In the years following the screening of the documentary, a number of historians have taken a closer look at the refusal mutiny of 21 September 1918 and tried to analyse the reasons for its occurrence. As has been shown, a host of potential causal factors were examined. These included the perceptions the men had of their own fighting abilities, their battle experiences, their conduct out of the line and whether or not they had been misled by a few 'bad eggs'. Indecisive leadership and confusing messages must also be seen as relevant in the confused commotion of the battlefield situation that existed at that time. The mutiny may never have eventuated had the leadership at that time been more proactive.

Despite the previous war experiences of the mutineers, there is always a tendency for observers to question the courage of men who were charged with mutiny and gaoled for desertion. Slowly but surely, the medical authorities have come to realise that men who were previously seen as malingerers were actually suffering from shellshock. Historical analysis has shown that many of the mutineers, despite having previously rendered excellent service, were, at the time of the mutiny, war weary. Their bank deposits of courage were dangerously low.

The only certainty to arise out of all this discussion is that there is no single factor that all external observers agree was the sole cause of the drastic action taken by the men. That is the nature of historical analysis. The beauty of historical analysis lies in the fact that it makes possible a better understanding of why the men did what they did. As a result of this, each observer can make a more informed decision as to whether or not the men deserved to be shunned, shamed and ostracised, or regarded more sympathetically.

For this observer, had these men been provided with more effective leadership rather than being subjected to conflicting messages in an environment marked by noise and confusion while they were suffering from war weariness and fatigue, the outcome could have been different. They needed someone who would listen to their complaints but who would then cajole them and persuade them rather than just dismiss their grievances out of hand.

These men had shown resilience, albeit in varying degrees. Some of the group had been rewarded for their gallantry, and others were about to be. All of them had previously experienced battlefront conditions, although some had handled it better than others. Many of the group had reached their 'tipping point'. In other words, the group was made up of individuals, and it is up to each individual observer to decide how to view the behaviour of these men in terms of the background from which the mutiny arose. It is only through examining the background of the men and the circumstances in which they were placed that an observer can form some degree of empathy for them.

The 'mutineers', the men who were found guilty of and gaoled for desertion just as the Great War was drawing to a close, were just like every other soldier who fought on the Western Front in at least one respect. They would not have looked back fondly on their days at the battlefront. Many of their comrades would also have done things of which they were not proud. The difference is that in some of those instances, they were not found out; they only had their own consciences to answer to.

At the end of the first volume of his official history of the war, Charles Bean asked, 'What was the dominant force that motivated them [the men of the AIF]?' He then answered his own question by saying, 'It lay in the mettle of the men themselves.'[6]

There is no doubt that, in general, the men of the AIF who returned to Australia had a vastly different perception of what war was about than the overly optimistic view that many of them held at the start of the war. Many of the men also changed. For some, the changes were subtle, but for others, they were devastating. They may have fought in the same war, but each man also fought his own personal battle.

Having lived for so long with Death, they now wanted to get on with Life.

ROLLO TAPLIN: HOMECOMING AND LIFE

Rollo Taplin's homecoming would have mirrored that of thousands of his comrades, but with one significant difference. Like them, he would have been pleased to be reunited with his family members, especially his sister, who had provided him with a place to live before he enlisted. He, too, was reluctant to talk about the war, the friends who were no longer alive and the terrible conditions that he had endured on the Western Front. He did not even talk much about his bravery commendation, or the fact that it had not led to an actual award.

Unlike the vast majority of his former comrades, however, he always had one thought nagging at the back of his mind. How much did his family and friends know, if anything, about the way the war had ended for him? Did people know anything about his imprisonment? If they did not, would there come a time when they did find out about it? How should he deal with that situation? Should he tell them everything now and risk the possibility of them thinking less of him?

As it turned out, his family knew nothing about the court martial, its verdict and his imprisonment. He never revealed this chapter of his life to them, choosing to keep it to himself. This resolve continued over the years, even when he met and later married his wife. Nor did he tell the story to his children, or their children. He never marched on Anzac Day, but in this he was no different from many others who had returned from wars. For them, occasions such as Anzac Day were too overwhelming, bringing back unwanted memories. He always said that the reason was that he had marched enough when he was in the army and didn't ever want to march again.

Nor was Rollo Taplin's secret ever unintentionally revealed by others who knew of his involvement. His role in the mutiny never appeared in any newspaper article. It was eventually revealed by the distinctive nature of his voice. He was approached to make a comment for the war documentary *Mutiny on the Western Front*, and gave his consent on the condition that he retained his anonymity. He would never have considered the possibility of his own family members recognising his voice when they watched the documentary. When they questioned him as to whether or not it was his voice, he admitted that it was, and so his secret was finally revealed 60 years after his arrival back in Australia.

Rollo Taplin was a deeply religious man. His Roman Catholic faith was important to him, and it is likely that this faith helped him to live with his secret and the associated guilt of keeping such a secret. He was also a loving, caring man, and for this he was in turn deeply loved and admired by his family. He died in 1981, but is still fondly remembered by his children and grandchildren.

He was also a forgiving man. Unlike many of his former comrades, he never harboured any resentment against the Germans. He would later joke with his grandchildren, calling them 'dummkopf' and explaining that this was the German word for 'blockhead'.

However, despite his English ancestry, he often spoke of the incompetence of the English officers. Once again, in doing this, he was no different from many who fought in the war, as well as others who later made a study of the tactics used during the war. As has been shown, he did retain a particularly strong dislike, or distaste, or perhaps even something stronger for those who, as he saw it, did not adequately deal with the situation that arose on 21 September 1918. He did not see his actions and those of his comrades as the actions of men who were shirkers. They were men who could have been reasoned with and persuaded. However, apart from Captain Moffatt, nobody really bothered.

The outlook adopted by Rollo Taplin, which was to guide him for the rest of his life, is encapsulated in an incident that occurred soon after his return from England. He bumped into Joe Weber, an old school friend, and at first Joe looked away, until Rollo walked up to him and said 'hello'. Joe had been worried that Rollo would not talk to him, as he was of German ancestry, his mother being German and his father having been born in Australia to German parents.

Rollo told Joe that this was of no significance; they were friends, and would remain so. He had no animosity towards Germans.

It was through his friendship with Joe that Rollo was to meet his future wife. Rollo joined Joe and his friends on outings and picnics and became attracted to Joe's only sister Amelia. They courted for some time before marrying in 1925, and their wedding ceremony reflected the devout Catholic outlook they shared. The service was conducted at St Thomas' Church in Lewisham by the Right Reverend Monsignor E. Brauer, Rector of St. Columba's College in Springwood, who was assisted in the Nuptial Mass by the Very Reverend Father T. Phelan, Parish Priest and Chancellor of the Archdiocese of Sydney. The bride was greeted at the main porch of the church by more than 30 Children of Mary. After the wedding reception, the couple left for their honeymoon in the Blue Mountains.

Their marriage was blessed by the arrival of a son in 1926 and two daughters in 1934 and 1935. Rollo Taplin had trained as a carpenter, and was becoming successful in his trade, so he and Amelia were able to save up and buy their first home.

However, once again, circumstances were to conspire against him. With the arrival of the Great Depression, he found himself a creditor of people who were either unwilling or unable to pay him the money they owed him. As a consequence, he was unable to meet his own debts and, in 1930, was declared bankrupt. A grandson who has compiled much of the family's history still has a cheque made out to Rollo Taplin that bounced in 1929.

A copy of the bounced check

Rollo and Amelia lost their house and were obliged to move in with Amelia's parents in Summer Hill. Rollo eked out a living by going from door to door offering his services as a handyman. After a couple of years, he was able to secure a job at Shell's Clyde refinery as a handyman. This gave him the economic security that he had probably never had in his lifetime, and he remained in their employ until his retirement.

Working for Shell also enabled Rollo and Amelia to finally buy their own home. This was in Ashbury, and it was here that Rollo built a work-shed where he used to do his woodworking. He also grew vegetables and ran a small chook pen. For he and many like him, these were not just hobbies. They were also a means of making their incomes go further. The Great Depression taught this lesson to many. His grandchildren recalled the interesting smells of compost and wood shavings that came from the garden area and shed, respectively.

Rollo Taplin also pursued interests outside the family home. He regularly attended church and was a member of the St Vincent de Paul Society. This involved visiting needy families to deliver food parcels and provide them with hope for the future.

It would seem that he never forgot the hope and support given to him by others, such as his sister, during the years preceding his enlistment, when all had seemed bleak. He was aged 84 at the time of his death in 1981.

APPENDICES

APPENDIX I

DEATH SENTENCES AND EXECUTIONS IN WORLD WAR I

It should be noted that none of these national totals include victims of summary executions carried out without recourse to a court martial.

Nation	Number of Death Sentences	Number of Men Executed	% of Death Sentences Carried Out
Italy	4028	750	19
Great Britain	3118	361	12
France	2500	650	26
Austria-Hungary	1175	1148	98
Canada	222	25	11
Belgium	200	12	6
Germany	150	48	32
USA	145	35	24
Australia	121	0	0
New Zealand	28	5	18
South Africa	11	1	9
Russia	unknown		

| Japan | | 0 | |

Source: http://www.encyclopedia.1914-1918-online.net/article/military_justice, p.10, retrieved 22 May 2015.

APPENDIX 2

EXECUTIONS IN THE BRITISH ARMY, 1914–1918

It should be noted that the vast majority of these executions were for offences committed on the Western Front.

Executions by Offence	Total	Executio
Desertion	245	
Cowardice	17	
Quitting Post	7	
Disobedience	5	
Murder	19	
Striking a superior officer	4	
Casting away arms	2	
Mutiny	3	
Sleeping on post	2	
	304	

Note: The largest single category was 'Desertion'. There was a considerable number of other offences that would have had a similar impact on the availability of troops for battle but that were recorded differently. These include: Absence, 37,004; Insubordination and

Disobedience, 22,891; Self-inflicted wounds, 3894; and Drunkenness, 35,313.

Source: Butler, Colonel Arthur Graham, *Official History of the Australian Army Medical Services, 1914–918*, Vol. III, "Special Problems and Services", 1st edition, 1943, p.90.

APPENDIX 3

MUTINEER AND NON-MUTINEER OCCUPATIONS

Comparison of the occupations of mutineers and non-mutineers in 1st Battalion, September 1918

Occupation	Non-mutineers %	Mutineers %
Professional	5.33	0
Clerical	11.33	4.03
Tradesman	14	15.32
Labourer	18.66	33.87
Industrial and manufacturing	11.33	13.7
Transport	8	7.25
Commercial	3.33	2.41
Rural	18	12.9
Seafaring	2	2.41
Mining	0.66	4.03
Domestic	4	2.41
Other/Unstated	3.33	3.21

Source: Blair, Dale, Dinkum Diggers: An Australian Battalion at War, Melbourne University Press, 1997, p.161.

APPENDIX 4

ALLIED FORMATIONS IN WORLD WAR I

Army: Three or four corps under the command of a general (180,000–320,000 men)

Army Corps: Three to four divisions under the command of a lieutenant general (60,000–80,000 men)

Division: Three brigades along with artillery under the command of a major general (20,000 men)

Brigade: Four battalions commanded by a brigadier general or brigadier (4000 men)

Battalion: Four companies commanded by a lieutenant colonel (1000 men)

Company: Four platoons commanded by a captain (200 men)

Platoon: Four sections commanded by a lieutenant and assisted by a sergeant (32–40 men)

Section: Eight to ten men commanded by a corporal

APPENDIX 5

TERRITORIAL RECRUITMENT AND DIVISIONAL STRUCTURE FOR THE 1ST DIVISION OF THE AIF IN WORLD WAR I

1st Division

> 1st Brigade
> *1st–4th Battalions NSW*
> 2nd Brigade
> *5th–8th Battalions Vic*
> 3rd Brigade
> *9th Battalion Qld*
> *10th and 11th Battalions SA*
> *12th Battalion Tas (and WA and SA)*
> **Source:** Jonathan King, The Western Front Diaries: The Anzacs' Own Story, Battle by Battle, Simon & Schuster, Australia, Pty. Ltd, 2008, p.589.

APPENDIX 6

AUSTRALIAN 1ST DIVISION COMMANDERS DURING WORLD WAR I

Major General William T. Bridges
6 August 1914 to 15 May 1915

Brigadier General H.B. Walker
15 May 1915 to 24 June 1915

Major General J. Gordon Legge
24 June 1915 to 26 July 1915

Brigadier General H.B. Walker
26 July 1915 to 13 October 1915

Brigadier General J.J. Talbot Hobbs
13 October 1915 to 6 November 1915

Brigadier General/Major General Harry Chauvel
6 November 1915 to 14 March 1916

Major General H.B. Walker
14 March 1916 to 31 May 1918

Major General T. William Glasgow
31 May 1918 to November 1918

Source: Jonathan King, The Western Front Diaries: The Anzacs' Own Story, Battle by Battle, Simon & Schuster, Australia Pty. Ltd., 2008, p.588.

APPENDIX 7

COMMAND STRUCTURE, 1ST BATTALION AIF AS AT 21ST SEPTEMBER 1918

GOC 1st Division

Major General Sir Thomas William Glasgow (AIF, from Queensland)

GOC 1st Brigade

Brigadier General Iven Gifford Mackay (AIF, from NSW).

Temporary (6 June 1918 – 11 November 1918)

Commanding Officer 1st Battalion

Lieutenant Colonel Bertie Vandeleur Stacy (17 March 1917 – 13 January 1919)

Regimental Medical Officer: Captain Edwin Thomas Cato

D Company

Captain Charles William Somerset (June 1918)

Lieutenant George Steen (Temporary captain: 14 July 1918)

Platoon Commanders

Lieutenant Hubert Victor Chedgey (May 1918)

Lieutenant Claude Ronald Morley (June 1918)

Lieutenant George Edward Gaskell (June 1918)

Lieutenant Wesley Merwyn Blake (September 1918)

Source: Dr Roger Lee, Head of the Australian Army History Unit and Army Historian.

APPENDIX 8

BATTLES IN WHICH THE AUSTRALIAN CORPS WAS INVOLVED IN FRANCE IN 1918

Hebuterne	March 27 – April 5
First Dernancourt	March 28
First Morlancourt	March 28–30
First Villers-Bretonneaux	April 4
Second Dernancourt	April 5
Hangard Wood	April 7
Hazebrouck	April 14, April 17
Zeebruge	April 22–23
Second Villiers-Bretonneaux	April 24–25
Second Morlancourt	May 4–9
Ville-sur-Ancre	May 19
Third Morlancourt	June 10
Hamel	July 4
Amiens	August 8
Lihons	August 9–11
Etinehem	August 10–13
Proyart	August 10–12
Lille	August 16–17

Chuignes	August 23
Mont St Quentin	August 31 – September 2
Hindenburg Outpost Line	September 18
St Quentin Canal	September 29 – October 1
Montbrehain	October 5

Note: Members of the 1st Battalion were involved in a great number of the battles listed above, but not all of them.

Source: *'Beaucoup Australiens ici': The Australian Corps in France, 1918,* researched and written by Dr Richard Reid (with assistance from Courtney Page and Robert Pounds) on behalf of the Commonwealth Government of Australia for the 80th anniversary of the ending of World War 1, revised edition, November, 2000, p.75.

References

Chapter 1: They went with songs to the battle...

[1] Gammage, W., *The Broken Years*, Penguin, Melbourne, 1992, quoted in Images of Australian History, G. Nicholls, M. Emmelkamp, F. Prince, A. Pollock, Thomas Nelson, Melbourne, p.182.

[2] *'Mawson's Men at the Front'*, The Argus (Melbourne), 23 December 1915: p.7, retrieved 16 April 2014 from [https://nla.gov.au/nla.news-article1587572]

[3] RABAUL, (1914, October 6). *The Sydney Morning Herald*, (NSW 1842–1954), p.6, Retrieved 20 June 2013 from [https://nla.gov.au/nla.news-article15536352]

[4] NAA: B2455 Series, Rollo Taplin service records and family historical records.

Chapter 2: The Real War and the Propaganda War

[1] Gammage, W., *The Broken Years*, Penguin, Melbourne, 1992, quoted in Images of Australian History, G. Nicholls, M.

Emmelkamp, F. Prince, A. Pollock, (Thomas Nelson, Australia), p.20.

[2] *Flogging Germans, New Guinea, 30 November 1914 [Proclamation Graphic]*, Australian Light Horse Studies Centre, 5 January 2010. Retrieved 5 March 2013 from [https://alhresearch.tripod.com/Light_Horse/index.blog?topic_id=1106539]

[3] Mackenzie, Seaforth S., *The Australians at Rabaul*, Official History of Australia in the War of 1914–1918, edited by C.E.W. Bean, Vol. X, 8th edition, Sydney, Angus and Robertson, 1940, p.262.

[4] Ibid., p.261.

[5] For a fuller discussion of this incident, see Australia's Real Baptism of Fire: Heroes Known Only to a Few by Greg Raffin, Five Senses Education, 2014.

[6] Gammage, W., op. cit., pp.16–17.

[7] NAA: B2455 Series, Rollo Taplin service records.

Chapter 3: Birth of a Legend

[1] Butler, Colonel Arthur Graham, *Special Problems and Services*, Official History of the Australian Army Medical Services,

1914–1918, Vol. III, 1st Edition, 1943, p.889.

[2] Bean, C.E.W., 'The Australian Imperial Force in France during the Allied Offensive, 1918', in Official History of Australia in the War of 1914–1918, edited by C.E.W. Bean, Vol. VI, Angus and Robertson, 1942, pp.5–6. Located at https://www.AWM.GOV.AU/COLLECTION/rcdig1069690/, Retrieved 3 February 2016.

[3] King, Jonathan, Gallipoli Diaries: The Anzacs' Own Story Day by Day, Kangaroo Press, 2003, p.4.

[4] [https://acms.sl.nsw.gov.au/_transcript/2011/D11976/a2748.htm], Retrieved 22 May 2015.

[5] Blair, Dale, Dinkum Diggers: An Australian Battalion at War, Melbourne University Press, 1997, pp.164–5.

[6] [https://www.awm.gov.au/units/unit-11188/] Retrieved 15 June 2014.

[7] NAA: Series B2455, SERN 2700 Pte W.J. Robson; NAA: Series B2455, SERN 1382 L/Cpl R. Beggs;

NAA: Series B2455, SERN 1118 Pte W. Case;

NAA: Series B2455, SERN 1715 Pte E.F. Stokes;

NAA: Series B2455, SERN 2606 Pte A. Lawrence;

NAA: Series B2455, SERN 550 Cpl J. Brissett.
[8] King, Jonathan, Gallipoli Diaries: The Anzacs' Own Story Day by Day, Kangaroo Press, 2003, p.127.
[9] NAA: Series B2455, SERN 2177 Pte A. Mullins.
[10] Stated by Peter Stanley in an email to the author, 3 January 2017.

Chapter 4: Military Training and Discipline

[1] Lord Moran, *The Anatomy of Courage*, Constable, London, 1945, p. x.
[2] Sir Peter Cosgrove, quoted with permission from personal correspondence with the author, 13 July 2015.
[3] Lord Moran op. cit., p.177.
[4] Ibid., p.197.
[5] Ibid., p.70.
[6] Ibid., p.115.
[7] Ibid., p.134.
[8] Ibid., pp.152–3.
[9] Diary entry by Captain E.A. Warren, 27th Btn, 17 October 1915, quoted in

Bill Gammage, *The Broken Years, Australian Soldiers in the Great War*, Melbourne University Press, 2010, p.89.
[10] Lord Moran, op. cit., pp 156–7.
[11] [https://en.wikipedia.org/wiki/List_of_New_Zealand_soldiers_executed_during_World_War_], Retrieved 6 May 2014.
[12] Butler, Colonel Arthur Graham, *Special Problems and Services*, in Official History of the Australian Army Medical Services, 1914–1918, Vol. III, (1st Edition, 1943, p.74.
[13] [http://www.awm.gov.au/encyclopedia/desertion/], Retrieved 6 May 2014.
[14] Pedersen, Peter, *The Anzacs: Gallipoli to the Western Front*, Penguin Books, 2007, p.304.
[15] Carlyon, Les, *The Great War*, Pan Macmillan Australia Pty Ltd, 2006, pp.475–7.
[16] Stanley, Peter, *Bad Characters: Sex, Crime, Mutiny, Murder and the Australian Imperial Force*, Murdoch Books Pty Ltd, 2010, p.174.
[17] Pedersen, Peter, 'Thou Shalt Not Kill.' [http://www.diggerhistory.info/pages-discipline/details.htm] p.2, Retrieved 15 May 2015.

Chapter 5: Dealing with the Realities

[1] Dexter, Chaplain W.E., in Michael McKernan. *Padre, Australian Chaplains in Gallipoli and France,* Allen and Unwin, Sydney, 1986 quoted in King, Jonathan, *Gallipoli Diaries: The Anzacs Own Story Day by Day,* Kangaroo Press, 2003, p.57.

[2] Butler, Colonel Arthur Graham, *Special Problems and Services,* in Official History of the Australian Army Medical Services, 1914–1918, Vol. III, (1st Edition, 1943), p.886. Retrieved 23 May 2015 from [htps://www.awm.gov.au/histories/first_world_war/AWMOHWW1/AAMS/Vol13/]

[3] Ibid., p.889 ([http://www.awm.gov.au/collection/RCDIG1069847/]), Retrieved 9 February 2016.

[4] NAA: Series B2455, SERN 3490 R.C. Taplin; NAA: Series B2455, SERN 2978 J.J. Couley.

[5] NAA: Series B2455, SERN 3407 L/Cpl C.W. Muir;

NAA: Series B2455, SERN 3064 L/Cpl D.W. Humphreys;

NAA: Series B2455, SERN 2876 Pte M. Mackey;

NAA: Series B2455, SERN 2700 Pte W.J. Robson;

NAA: Series B2455, SERN 1229 Pte A.S. Barclay;

NAA Series B2455, SERN 2177 Pte A. Mullins;

NAA: Series B2455, SERN 2606 Pte A. Lawrence;

NAA: Series B2455, SERN 3522 Pte A. Woodford;

NAA: Series B2455, SERN 948 Lieutenant J.C. Hayes;

NAA: Series B2455, SERN 3801 L/Cpl E.M. Porter;

NAA: Series B2455, SERN 3966 Cpl R.H.C. McKay;

NAA: Series B2455, SERN 3812 L/Cpl L.W. Pettit;

NAA: Series B2455, SERN 2562 L/Cpl E.A. Besley;

NAA: Series B2455, SERN 2928 L/Cpl E. Walker; NAA: Series B2455, SERN 3563 Cpl R. Cooney.

[6] L/Cpl J. Cohen 24th Btn, written 29 July 1916, quoted in Gammage, Bill, The Broken Years: Australian Soldiers in the Great War, Melbourne University Press, 2010, p.170.

[7] Ibid., written 31 July 1916, quoted in Gammage, Bill, op. cit., p.172.

[8] Bean, C.E.W., 'The Australian Imperial Force in France during the Allied Offensive, 1918' in *The Official History of Australia in the War of 1914–1918*, edited by C.E.W. Bean, Vol. VI, Angus and Robertson, 1942, pp.871–2.

[9] Barwick, Archie, *In Great Spirits: The World War I Diary of Archie Barwick from Gallipoli to the Western Front and Home Again*, Harper Collins, 2013, p.131.

[10] Ibid., p.133.

[11] NAA: Series B2455, Rollo Taplin.

[12] Barwick, Archie, op. cit., p.290.

[13] Price, B.J., Phillips, R.S. and Walshe, R.D., *A History of the World and Australia in the Twentieth Century*, Hogbin and Poole, 1965, p.22.

[14] Butler, Colonel Arthur, op. cit., p.897.

[15] Ibid., p.81.

[16] Ibid., pp.100–101.

[17] Ibid., p.942.

[18] Ibid., p.899.

[19] Thompson, Alastair, *Anzac Memories: Living with the Legend*, Monash University Publishing, 2013, p.46.

[20] Alastair Thompson's book, quoted here, includes an extensive discussion

on the topic of war gratuities and pensions. Among other things, it shows that the government authorities continued not to fully understand the ongoing problems of those who suffered mental health issues as a result of their involvement in the war.

[21]　Ibid., p.47.
[22]　Ibid., p.48.
[23]　Lt. Robert Hunter 2nd Btn, 15 October 1915, quoted in Gammage Bill, op. cit., p.118.
[24]　Lt. Eric Chinner 32nd Btn, 15 July 1916, quoted in Gammage, Bill, op. cit., p.163.
[25]　Lt. Grubb, 14 September 1915, quoted in Gammage, Bill, op. cit., p.111.
[26]　Barwick, Archie, op. cit., p.185.
[27]　Butler Colonel Arthur, op. cit., p.887.

Chapter 6: Mutiny and Desertion

[1]　Barwick, Archie, *In Great Spirits: The World War I Diary of Archie Barwick from Gallipoli to the Western Front and Home Again*, Harper Collins, 2013, p.282.
[2]　RIOTING. (1916, February 15), *The Sydney Morning Herald* (NSW: 1842–1954), p.9, retrieved 15 June 2015

from [https://nla.gov.au/nla.news-article15646740].

This episode is also discussed at some length in: Stanley, Peter, *Bad Characters: Sex, Crime, Mutiny, Murder and the Australian Imperial Force*, Murdoch Books Pty Ltd, 2010, pp.59–60.

[3] [https://en.wikipedia.org/wiki/%C3%89taplesMutiny], Retrieved 15 June 2015.

[4] Bean, C.E.W., *The A.I.F. in France 1918*, Official History of Australia in the War of 1914–1918, edited by C.E.W. Bean, Vol. VI, Angus and Robertson, 1942, pp.938–39.

[5] Ibid., p.940.

[6] Ekins, Ashley, 'Fighting to Exhaustion: Morale, Discipline and Combat Effectiveness in the Armies of 1918', in 1918 Year of Victory: The End of the Great War and the Shaping of History, Exisle Publishing, 2010, Chapter 7, p.21.

[7] Ekins, Ashley, ibid., p.22.

[8] Carlyon, Les, The Great War, Pan Macmillan, Australia, 2006, p.693.

[9] Ekins, Ashley, op. cit., p.23.

[10] Bean, C.E.W., op. cit., p.875.

[11] [https://www.awm.gov.au/atwar/ww1/] Retrieved 9 February 2016.

[12]   London Gazette, 27 June 1917, p.6382, position 1; Commonwealth of Australia Gazette, 11 October 1917, p.2663, position 95. This particular battle and act of valour are discussed in some detail by Jonathan King in The Western Front Diaries: The Anzacs' Own Story Battle by Battle, Simon & Schuster, Australia, 2008, pp.273–288.

[13]   [https://en.wikipedia.org/wiki/First_Australian_Imperial_Force...,V] Retrieved 24 March 2016]

[14]   Jonathan King, op. cit., pp.360–61.

[15]   NAA: B2455 Series, SERN 3490 Cpl R.C. Taplin.

[16]   War Diary, 1st Brigade, 1st Australian Division Anzac Corps, 10 May 1917, recommendation for 2978 Pte James Couley.

[17]   NAA: Series B2455, SERN 2978 Pte J.J. Couley.

[18]   NAA: Series B2455, SERN 3354 3787 Pte W. Martin.

[19]   NAA: Series B2455, SERN 2928 L/Cpl E. Walker.

[20]   Ross Coulthart, Charles Bean, Harper Collins, 2014, p.284.

[21]   Mackenzie, John, A Disabling Minority: Mutiny in the First Battalion AIF,

September, 1918, unpublished BA Honours thesis, University College, Australian Defence Force Academy, 1988, p.67.

[22] NAA: Series B2455, SERN 7350 Pte A. Barnett.

[23] NAA: Series B2455, SERN 1118 Pte W. Case.

[24] NAA: Series B2455, SERN 7475 Pte E. Dick.

[25] NAA: Series B2455, SERN 6004 Pte A. Ellis.

[26] NAA: Series B2455, SERN 3490 Cpl R. Taplin.

[27] NAA: Series B2455, SERN 2562 L/Cpl E. Besley.

[28] Monash, General Sir John, *The Australian Victories in France in 1918*, Angus and Robertson, 1936, pp.257–9. Professor Peter Stanley expressed his scepticism about these statistics in a comment made to the author.

[29] AWM4 Australian Imperial Force unit war diaries, 1914–1918 War, Infantry, Item Number 23/18/34, 1st Infantry Battalion, August 1918. C.E.W. Bean, *The A.I.F. in France in 1918*, Official History of Australia in the War of 1914–1918, edited by C.E.W. Bean,

Volume VI, Angus and Robertson, 1942, pp.650–652.

The citation for the Distinguished Conduct Medal can be found in the service records for both Sergeant Hayes and Lieutenant Andrews: NAA: Series B2455, SERN 3232 Lieutenant Andrews; NAA: Series B2455, SERN 948 J.C. Hayes. This incident was also written about by Ross McMullin in the article *Salute to the 1st Battalion* in the Adelaide Advertiser, 11 August 1998.

[30]　NAA: Series B2455, SERN 3563 R. Cooney.

[31]　NAA: Series B2455, SERN 2928 E. Walker.

[32]　NAA: Series B2455, SERN 1118 Pte W. Case.

　　NAA: Series B2455, SERN 1715 Pte E. Stokes.

[33]　Williams H.R., Comrades of the Great Adventure, (Sydney, 1935), p.289, quoted by Bill Gammage in *The Broken Years: Australian soldiers in the Great War*, Melbourne University Press, 2010, p.206.

Chapter 7: The Mutiny on the Western Front

[1] Butler, Colonel Arthur Graham, *Special Problems and Services*, in Official History of the Army Medical Services, 1914–1918, Vol. III, (1st Edition, 1943), p.723, retrieved on 23 May 1915 from [https://www.awm.gov.au/histories/first_world_war/AWMOHWWI/AAMS/Vol13/]

[2] AWM 28, Recommendation Files for Honours and Awards, AIF, 1914–1918 War, *For Citation in Corps Orders for Gallantry and Devotion to duty during operations on 23/8/18*, 1st A I Brigade, 1st Australian Division, Australian Corps.[https://www.awm.gov.au/people/rolls/R1616129/], Retrieved 4 May 2015.

[3] Mackenzie, John, *A Disabling Minority: Mutiny in the First Battalion AIF, September, 1918*, unpublished BA Honours thesis, University College, Australian Defence Force Academy, 1988, p.45. This is the only study that I drew upon that dealt solely with the mutiny of 21 September 1918.

[4] C.E.W. Bean, *The A.I.F. in France in 1918*, Official History of Australia in the War

of 1914–1918, edited by C.E.W. Bean, Volume VI, Angus and Robertson, 1942, p.933. Downloaded from [www.awm.gov.au]

[5] Stacy, B.V., *Report on Operations of 20–21 September 1918, Appendix 11*, p.46 in 1st Infantry Battalion War Diary, September 1918, AWM RCDIG1008895, Item Number 23/18/35. Downloaded from [www.awm.gov.au]

[6] [https://recordsearch.naa.gov.au/SearchNRetrieve/Interface/Viewimage.aspx?B=209393], Retrieved 4 May 2015.

[https://recordsearch.naa.gov.au/SearchNRetrieve/Interface/ViewImage.aspx?B=3900026], Retrieved 14 April 2016.

A good narrative account of the events of the mutiny and the ensuing courts martial can be found in Mackenzie, op. cit. and E.J. Garstang, Crime and Punishment on the Western Front: The Australian Imperial Force and British Army Discipline, unpublished PhD thesis, Murdoch University, 2009. All efforts to seek approval to quote from the Garstang thesis proved unsuccessful.

[7] Bean, C.E.W., *The AIF in France in 1918*, Official History of Australia in the War of 1914–1918, edited by C.E.W. Bean,

Vol. VI, Angus and Robertson, 1942, p.934.

Stacy, B.V., *Report on Operations of 20–21 September 1918, Appendix 11*, pp.46–48, in 1st Infantry Battalion War Diary, September 1918, AWM RCDIG1008895, Item Number 23/18/35. Downloaded from [www.awm.gov.au]

[8] [https://recordsearch.naa.gov.au/SearchN Retrieve/Interface/Viewimage.aspx?B==20 9393], pp.10–15, Retrieved 4 May 2015.

[9] 1st Battalion AIF Field General Court martial of Cpl (3661) George F. Wethered held on 16 October 1918; Field General Court martial of Lance Sergeant (335) Milton Hasthorpe held on 15 October 1918.

[10] 1st Battalion AIF Field General Court martial. Joint trial of five non-commissioned officers and 29 privates of D Company.

Stacy, B.V., *Report on Operations of 20–21 September 1918, Appendix 11*, pp.46–48, in 1st Infantry Battalion War Diary, September 1918, AWM RCDIG1008895, Item Number 23/18/35. Downloaded from [www.awm.gov.au]

[11] NAA: Series B2455, SERN 6327 Pte H.H. Tickner.

[12] Garstang, E.J., op. cit., pp.148–49.
[13] 1st Battalion AIF Field General Court martial. Joint trial of 13 privates of B Company.
[14] 1st Battalion AIF Field General Court martial. Joint trial of 19 members of A Company. Garstang, E.J., op. cit., pp.161–162.
[15] Stanley, Peter, Bad Characters: Sex, Crime, Mutiny, Murder and the Australian Imperial Force, Murdoch Books Pty Ltd, 2010, p.210.
[16] Blair, Dale, Dinkum Diggers: An Australian Battalion at War, Melbourne University Press, 1997, p.157.
[17] NAA: Series B2455, SERN 6004 Pte A.J. Ellis;
NAA: Series B2455, SERN 7472 Pte H.S. Clarke;
NAA: Series B2455, SERN 7738 W.J. Holmes;
NAA: Series B2455, SERN Cpl (550) J. Brisset.
[18] Mackenzie, J.J., op. cit., p.36.
[19] Ibid., p.27.

Chapter 8: Isolated and Lonely but not Alone

[1] Mackenzie, John, *A Disabling Minority: Mutiny in the First Battalion AIF, September 1918*, unpublished BA Honours thesis, University College, Australian Defence Force Academy, 1988, pp.65–6.

[2] Garstang, Edward, *Crime and Punishment on the Western Front: The Australian Imperial Force and British Army Discipline*, unpublished PhD thesis, Murdoch University, 2009, p.166.

[3] Blair, Dale, *Dinkum Diggers: An Australian Battalion at War*, Melbourne University Press, 1997, p.162.

[4] Transcript from documentary *Mutiny on the Western Front*, Mingara Films Pty Ltd, 1979. The comments from Corporal Rollo Taplin were included in this documentary.

[5] NAA: Series B2455, SERN 1922 Pte W.H. Faulkner.

[6] NAA: Series B2455, SERN 6077 Pte A. Rook.

[7] NAA: Series B2455, SERN 1229 Pte A. Barclay.

[8]	Transcript from documentary *Mutiny on the Western Front*, Mingara Films Pty Ltd, 1979. Part of this reference was a comment made by the director, Richard Dennison, in an email to the author dated 1 April 2016.
[9]	Transcript from documentary *Mutiny on the Western Front*, Mingara Films Pty Ltd, 1979.
[10]	Mackenzie, J.J., op. cit., p.93.
[11]	Ekins, Ashley, *Fighting to Exhaustion: Morale, Discipline and Combat Effectiveness in the Armies of 1918*, in 1918 Year of Victory: The End of the Great War and the Shaping of History, Ashley Ekins, (editor), Angus and Robertson, 2008, p.271.
[12]	NAA: Series B2455, SERN 7350, Pte A. Barnett.
[13]	NAA: Series B2455, SERN 7754 Pte C.J. Johnstone.
[14]	NAA: Series B2455, SERN 7784 Pte R. Stafford.

Chapter 9: Nor the years condemn...

[1]	Bean, C.E.W., *The Australian Imperial Force in France during the Allied Offensive*

1918, in The Official History of Australia in the War of 1914–1918, Vol. VI, Angus & Robertson, 1942, pp.875–76.
[2] Ibid., p.877.
[3] Ibid., p.933.
[4] Ibid., p.933, pp.939–40.
[5] Mackenzie, John Joseph, *A Disabling Minority: Mutiny in the First Battalion AIF, September, 1918*, BA Honours thesis, Australian Defence Force Academy, 1988, p.48.
[6] Ibid., p.56.
[7] Ibid., p.62.
[8] Ibid., p.63.
[9] Ibid., p.66.
[10] Ibid., p.67.
[11] Ibid., p.65.
[12] Ibid., p.68.
[13] Ibid., pp.69–70.
[14] Ibid., p.69.
[15] NAA: Series B2455, SERN 7723 Pte James Earle.
[16] NAA: Series B2455, SERN 1118 Pte William Case.
[17] Mackenzie, op. cit., p.70.
[18] Ibid., p.84.
[19] Ibid., pp.88–89.

[20] Blair, Dale, *Dinkum Diggers: An Australian Battalion at War*, Melbourne University Press, 1997, p.163.
[21] Ibid., p.158.
[22] Ibid., p.160.
[23] Ibid., p.160.
[24] Garstang, Edward, *Crime and Punishment on the Western Front: The Australian Imperial Force and British Army Discipline*, PhD thesis, Murdoch University, 2009, p.40.
[25] Colonel A.G. Butler, *Special Problems and Services*, in Official History of the Australian Army Medical Services, 1914–1918, Vol. III (1st edition, 1943), p.900, pp.909–910.
[26] Blair, Dale, op. cit., p.162.
[27] Ibid., p.159.
[28] Ibid., pp.158–59.
[29] Ibid., p.160.
[30] Garstang, Edward, *Crime and Punishment on the Western Front: The Australian Imperial Force and British Army Discipline*, PhD thesis, Murdoch University, 2009, p.165. NB: Several unsuccessful attempts have been made to contact the author of this thesis. We apologise if there has been any infringement of

copyright and invite the copyright owner to contact us.

[31] Ibid., p.167.
[32] Ibid., p.176.
[33] Ekins, Ashley, *Fighting to Exhaustion: Morale, Discipline and Combat Effectiveness in the Armies of 1918*, in The Year of Victory: The End of the Great War and the Shaping of History, Exisle Publishing, 2010, Chapter 7, pp.15–16.
[34] Ibid., p.17.
[35] Ibid., pp.17–18.
[36] Ibid., p.28.
[37] Ibid., pp.29–30.
[38] Ibid., 30.
[39] Stanley, Peter, *Bad Characters: Sex, Crime, Mutiny, Murder and the Australian Imperial Force*, Murdoch Books, 2010, p.210.
[40] Ibid., p.210.
[41] Wise, Nathan, *Anzac Labour: Workplace Cultures in the Australian Imperial Force in the First World War*, Palgrave Macmillan, 2014, pp.86–7.
[42] Ibid., p.90.

Chapter 10: With the Benefit of Hindsight

[1] Lee, James J., The History of the First Battalion, AIF, 1914–1919, Sydney, 1931, p.110.

[2] [https://recordsearch.naa.gov.au/SearchNRetrieve/Interface/ViewImage.aspx?B=209393], p.12, Retrieved 4 May 2015.

[3] Blair, D.J., *Dinkum Diggers: An Australian Battalion at War*, Melbourne University Press, 1997, p.159.

[4] [https://recordsearch.naa.gov.au/SearchNRetrieve/Interface/ViewImage.aspx?B=209393], p.11, Retrieved 4 May 2015.

[5] Blair, D.J. op. cit., p.159.

[6] Ibid., p.161.

[7] Lindsay, Patrick, Fromelles: Australia's Darkest Hour and the Dramatic Discovery of Our Fallen World War One Diggers, Hardie Grant Books, 2008, p.66.

[8] McMullin, Ross, Pompey Elliott, Scribe Publications, 2002, pp.484–5.

[9] Ibid., p.96.

[10] Ibid., p.373, p.384.

[11] Transcript from documentary *Mutiny on the Western Front*, Mingara Films Pty Ltd, 1979.

[12] M. Lincoln and D.E. Lloyd, Stacy, Bertie Vandeleur (1886–1971)', Australian Dictionary of Biography. National Centre of Biography, Australian National University, https://adb. edu.au /biography/stacy-bertie-vandeleur-9235/ text15051, published first in hardcopy 1990, accessed 23 January 2017.

[13] Mackenzie, J.J., *A Disabling Minority: Mutiny in the First Battalion AIF, September, 1918*, BA Honours Thesis, Australian Defence Force Academy, 1988, pp.77–78.

[14] Blair, D.J. op. cit., pp.158–9.

Chapter 11: Life goes on ... to a conclusion

[1] T.H. Wintringham, quoted by Mackenzie, J.J., in A Disabling Minority: Mutiny in the First Battalion AIF, September, 1918, BA Honours thesis, Australian Defence Force Academy, 1988.

[2] Garstang, Edward John, *Crime and Punishment on the Western Front: The Australian Imperial Force and British Army*

Discipline, unpublished PhD thesis, Murdoch University, 2009, p.223. Several unsuccessful attempts have been made to contact this writer.

[3] Mackenzie, J.J., op. cit., p.28.

[4] Blair, Dale, *Dinkum Diggers: An Australian Battalion at War*, Melbourne University Press, 1997, p.162.

[5] Ibid., p.163.

[6] Bean C.E.W., *The Story of ANZAC from the Outbreak of the War to the End of the First Phase of the Gallipoli Campaign, May 4 1915*, Vol.1, Official History of Australia in the War of 1914–1918, edited by C.E.W. Bean, Angus & Robertson, 11th edition, 1941, pp.606–7. Downloaded from [www.awm.gov.au] on 4 October 2017.

BIBLIOGRAPHY

Books

Adam-Smith, Patsy, *The Anzacs*, Nelson, Melbourne, 1978.

Barwick, Archie, *In Great Spirits: The World War I Diary of Archie Barwick*, Harper Collins, 2013.

Bean, C.E.W., *The Story of ANZAC from the Outbreak of the War to the End of the First Phase of the Gallipoli Campaign, May 4 1915*, Vol.1, *Official History of Australia in the War of 1914–1918*, edited by C.E.W. Bean, Vol. VI, 8th Edition, Angus and Robertson, 1941.

Bean, C.E.W., 'The AIF in France 1918', *Official History of Australia in the War of 1914–1918*, edited by C.E.W. Bean, Vol. VI, 8th Edition, Angus and Robertson, 1942.

Blair, Dale, *Dinkum Diggers: An Australian Battalion at War*, Melbourne University Press, 1997.

Butler, Colonel Arthur Graham, *Official History of the Australian Army Medical Services, 1914–1918*,

Vol. III, 'Special Problems and Services', (1st Edition, 1943).

Carlyon, Les, *Gallipoli*, Pan Macmillan, Sydney, 2001. Carlyon, Les, *The Great War*, Pan Macmillan Australia Pty Ltd, 2006.

Coulthard-Clark, Chris, *The Encyclopaedia of Australia's Battles*, Allen & Unwin, Sydney, 1998.

Coulthart, Ross, *Charles Bean: If people really knew; one man's struggle to report the Great War and tell the truth*, Harper Collins Australia, 2014.

Coulthart, Ross, *The Lost Diggers*, Harper Collins Australia, 2012.

Ekins, Ashley, 'Fighting to Exhaustion: Morale, Discipline and Combat Effectiveness in the Armies of 1918', in *1918, Year of Victory: The End of the Great War and the Shaping of History*, Exisle Publishing, 2010.

Gammage, B., *The Broken Years: Australian Soldiers in the Great War*, Illustrated edition, Melbourne University Press, 2010.

Keegan, John, *The First World War*, Pimlico, London, 2002.

King, Jonathan, *The Western Front Diaries: The Anzacs' Own Story Battle by Battle*, Simon & Schuster Australia Pty Ltd, 2008.

King, Jonathan, *Gallipoli Diaries: The Anzacs Own Story Day by Day*, Kangaroo Press, 2003.

Lee, James J., *The History of the First Battalion*, Sydney, 1931.

Lindsay, Patrick, *Fromelles*, Hardie Grant, 2008.

Lindsay, Patrick, *The Spirit of the Digger*, Pan Macmillan, Sydney, 2004.

Mackenzie, Seaforth S., 'The Australians at Rabaul', *Official History of Australia in the War of 1914–1918*, edited by C.E.W. Bean, Vol. X, 8th Edition, Angus and Robertson, 1942.

McMullin, Ross, *Pompey Elliott*, Scribe Publications, Melbourne, 2002.

Monash, General Sir John, *The Australian Victories in France in 1918*, Angus and Robertson, 1936.

Moran, Lord, *The Anatomy of Courage*, Constable London, 1945.

Pedersen, Peter, *The Anzacs: Gallipoli to the Western Front*, Penguin Books, 2007.

Raffin Greg, *Australia's Real Baptism of Fire: Heroes Known Only To a Few*, Five Senses Education, 1914.

Robson, L., *The First AIF: A Study of its Recruitment 1914–1918*, Melbourne University Press, 1970.

Ross, J., *The Myth of the Digger*, Hale & Iremonger, Sydney, 1985.

Stanley, Peter, *Bad Characters: Sex, Crime, Mutiny, Murder and the Australian Imperial Force*, Murdoch Books Pty Ltd, 2010.

Thompson, Alastair, *Anzac Memories: Living with the Legend*, Monash University Publishing, 2013.

Ward, Russell, *The Australian Legend*, Oxford University Press, 1958.

Wise, Nathan, *Anzac Labour: Workplace Culture in the Australian Imperial Force during the First World War*, Palgrave Macmillan, 2014.

Articles and Theses

[No heading} *The Brisbane Courier (Qld. 1864–1933)* 12 July 1913: retrieved 24 November 2014 from [https://nla.gov.au/nla.newspage1578654]

'Mawson's Men at the Front', *The Argus (Melbourne)* 23 December 1915, p.7, retrieved 16 April 2014 from [https://nla.gov.au/nla.news-article1587572]

Dr Phillip Zimbardo, *The Banality of Heroism/Greater Good*, retrieved 5 July 2016, from [https://greatergood.berkeley.edu/article/item/the_banality_of_heroism]

Flogging Germans, German New Guinea, 30 November 1914 [Proclamation Graphic], Australian Light Horse Studies, 5 January 2010. Retrieved from [https://alh-research.tripod.com/Light_Horse/index.blog?topic_id=1106539]

Frewster, Kevin J., *Jacka, Albert (1893–1932)*, Australian Dictionary of Biography, National Centre of Biography, Australian National University, [https://adb.anu.edu.au/biography/jacka-albert-6808/text11779], accessed 15 June 2014.

Garstang, Edward John, *Crime and Punishment on the Western Front: The Australian Imperial Force and British Army Discipline*, PhD Thesis, Murdoch University, 2009.

Lindstrom, Richard, *The Australian Experience of Psychological Casualties, 1915–1939*, PhD thesis, Victorian University of Technology, 1997.

Mackenzie, John Joseph, *A Disabling Minority: Mutiny in the First Battalion AIF, September, 1918*, unpublished BA (Hons) thesis, Australian Defence Force Academy, 1988.

Pedersen, Peter, *Thou Shalt Not Kill*, [https://www.diggerhistory.info/pages-discipline/details.htm]

RABAUL, (1914, October 6), *The Sydney Morning Herald (NSW: 1842–1954)*, p.6, retrieved 20 June 2014 from [https://nla.gov.au/nla.nes-article15536352]

Rioting, (1916, February 15) *The Sydney Morning Herald (NSW 1842–1954)*, p.9, retrieved 15 June 2015 from [https://nla.gov.au/nla.news-article15646740]

Salute to the 1st Battalion, McMullin, Ross, *Adelaide Advertiser*, 11 August 1998.

Samuel Oliner in *Experts Look at What Causes Heroism*, [https://abcnews.go.com/health/story?id=117230], p.1, retrieved 22 December 2014.

Documentary Sources

'Glimpses of New Guinea', *Records of C.E.W. Bean: AWM38, 3DRL606 Folders*, Australian War Memorial AWM38, 3DRL606/258/11914-1927, p.50, [https://www.awm.gov.au/collection/records/awm38/3drl606-258-1.pdf], Retrieved 7 March 2014.

'Letter from O.W. Gillam to C.E.W. Bean, 30 March 1925', *Records of C.E.W. Bean: AWM38, 3DRL606 Folders*, Australian War Memorial, AWM383DRL606/258/1-1914-1927, p.20, [https://www.awm.gov.au/collection/records/awm38/3drl606/awm383drl606-258-1.pdf], Retrieved 7 March 2014.

AWM 28, *For Citation in Corps Orders for Gallantry and Devotion to Duty During Operations on 23/8/18*, 1st Australian Division, Australian Corps. *Recommendation Files for Honours and Awards, AIF, 1914–1918 War*, [https://www.awm.gov.au/peole/rolls/R1616129/], Retrieved 4 May 2015.

AWM4 Australian Imperial Force Unit War Diaries, 1914–1918 War, Infantry, Item Number 23/18/34, 1st Infantry Battalion.

Charles Bingham Elwell, Royal Navy Service Record, Kew, UK: The National Archive, Vol.8, Part 2, ADM 196/47/142.

Commonwealth of Australia Gazette, 11 October 1917

Commonwealth of Australia Gazette, various issues.
London Gazette, various issues.

NAA: Series A471, Barcode 209393, Court Martial Records of 5 NCOs of D Company.

NAA: Series A471, Barcode 3462767, Court Martial Records of 19 members of A Company.

NAA: Series A471, Barcode 6973787, Court Martial Records of 34 members of D Company.

NAA: Series A471, Barcode 7117456, Court Martial Records of 13 members of A Company.

NAA: Series A471, Barcode 7117509, Court Martial Records of Lance/Sgt M. Hasthorpe.

NAA: Series A471, Barcode 7277283, Court Martial Records of Cpl J. Brissett.

NAA: Series A471, Barcode 7877359, Court Martial Records of 45 members of C Company.

NAA: Series A471, Barcode 8196809, Court Martial Records of Cpl G.F. Wethered.

NAA: Series B2455, Individual Soldier Service Records (itemised in Footnotes).

The London Gazette, 11 July 1916, Supplement 29664.

The London Gazette, 27 June 1917.

The London Gazette, 28 January 1916, Supplement 29455.

War Diary, 1st Brigade, 1st Australian Division Anzac Corps.

Young, Sydney B., *War Diary 2 February – 1 September 1918*, State Library Collection of World War 1 Diaries, MLMSS 985/Item 6.

Documentaries, Family Histories and Websites

Mutiny on the Western Front, Mingara Films Pty Ltd, 1979.

Oral and family histories as itemised in the footnotes, e.g., the Taplin family.

Websites as itemised in the footnotes, e.g. the Australian War Memorial and National Archives of Australia websites.

Maps

AWM4 Australian Imperial Force War Diaries, 1914–18 War, 1st Infantry Battalion, September 1918, RCDIG 1008895, Item Number 23/18/35, pp.46–7. [https://www.awm.gov.au/collection/C13 47473], Retrieved 16 September 2017.

AWM4 Australian Imperial Force War Diaries, 1914–18 War, 1st Infantry Brigade, September 1918, Appendices RCDIG 1009361, AWM4-23/1/38Part2, pp.65–71.

ABOUT THE AUTHOR

Greg Raffin's early interest in history led to post-graduate studies in the subject and a lengthy career as a History Head teacher. In 2005 he was awarded the Premier's Military History scholarship and travelled to SE Asia to study the Burma-Siam "Death railway". He is also the author of, *Australia's real baptism of fire* which is an account of the Australian takeover of German possessions in New Guinea during the First World War.

Available now online or at all good bookstores

DUST DONKEYS AND DELUSIONS

The Myth of Simpson and his Donkey EXPOSED

Graham Wilson

***

View sample pages, reviews and more information on this and other titles at www.bigskypublishing.com.au

***

View sample pages, reviews and more information on this and other titles at www.bigskypublishing.com.au

323

BULLY BEEF & BALDERDASH VOLUME II

More myths of the AIF examined and debunked

Graham Wilson

***

View sample pages, reviews and more information on this and other titles at www.bigskypublishing.com.au

THE HELL PITS OF SENDRYU

A POW story of survival on the Death Railway and Nagasaki

JIM BRIGGINSHAW

***

View sample pages, reviews and more information on this and other titles at www.bigskypublishing.com.au

BACK COVER MATERIAL

Aurhor Greg Raffin considers what happens to men's hearts and minds in the course of a prolonged conflict like the Great War. This story, which will surprise readers – is not just about a group of exhausted and war weary Australian soldiers in 1918, it is a story about humanity in war: about what men do in war, and what war does to men.

On 21 September 1918, with retreating German forces on their last legs, the 1st Battalion of the AIF was ordered to return to the front just as they were being relieved and preparing for a well-earnt rest. It wasn't just the Germans who were on their last legs: the Australian were depleted and exhausted. In what was the largest such instance of mass 'combat refusal' in the AIF's history, the men of one company in the 1st Battalion defied the order. The 'mutiny' spread to other companies, and when the battalion did eventually comply with the order, over 100 men were absent.

The circumstance surrounding this mutiny have long been a matter of embarrassment for the AIF, and of fascination for military historians. While historians have approached the issue in purely military terms – the men as soldiers, over-extended service, rates of wounding, promotions, and so on – this book approach these 100 plus men as human beings. *Mutiny on the Western Front* trace how these events played out in the context of the exhausting demands placed upon a unit had seen practically continuous front-line action for not months, in war's final decisive stages.

Index

A
Andrews, Sergeant Dudley, *253*
Andrews, Harold, *208, 209*
Aylward, Corporal Albert, *247*

B
Bage, Edward, *18*
Barclay, Private Alan, *125*
Barnett, Private Anthony, *194*
Bean, Captain Charles, *5, 55, 58, 63, 73, 125, 129, 179, 182, 194, 208, 232, 238*
Beggs, Lance Corporal Richard, *68*
Berman, Private James, *238, 240*
Besley, Lance Corporal Ernest, *68, 125, 200, 247*
Birdwood, Lieutenant General William, *107, 143*
Blair, Dale, *60, 63, 73*
Bligh, Captain William, *164*
Bond, Lieutenant Thomas, *18, 20, 34*
Bootle, Captain John, *247, 253*
Braithwaite, Private Jack, *174*
Brissett, Corporal Joseph, *68, 266, 268*
Burnell, Frederick, *18*
Butler, Colonel Arthur, *99, 143, 200*

C
Case, Private William, *68, 194, 195, 209, 253*
Chauvel, General Harry, *185*
Churchill, Winston, PM, *81*
Clarke, Private Horace, *266*
Cooney, Corporal Roger, *125, 209, 238, 247*

Cosgrove, Sir Peter, *81, 86*
Couley, Private James, *91, 125, 187, 191, 209, 250*
Cox, Reverend William, *40, 42*

D
Dick, Private Charles, *195*

E
Earle, Private James, *240, 253*
Eitel, Private Conrad (aka Lionel Easton), *10, 18*
Elliott, Brigadier Harold, *179, 182*
Ellis, Private Arthur, *195, 266*

F
Fitzgerald, Admiral Charles, *45*

G
Glasgow, General Sir Thomas, *232*

H
Halsthate, Sergeant, *238*
Hasthorpe, Lance Sergeant Milton, *247, 250*
Hindenburg, General Paul von, *203*
Holmes, Colonel William, *36, 40, 42*
Holmes, Private William, *266*
Howell, Corporal George Julien, *185*
Hughes, Billy, PM, *137, 151*
Humphreys, Lance Corporal David Watkin, *125*

J
Jacka, Sergeant Albert, *34, 55, 143*
Johnson, Captain Eric, *247*

K
Keefe, Ernest, *173*
Keysor, Lieutenant Leonard, *63*

L
Lawrence, Private Arthur, *68, 125*

Ludendorff, General Erich, *203, 205*

M

Mackay, Brigadier General Iven, *261*
Mackenzie, John, *268*
Mackenzie, Captain Alexander, *187*
Mackey, Private Matthew, *125*
Marsh, Agnes, *20*
Martin, Private Walter, *191*
Mawson, Sir Douglas, *18*
McDonald, Major George, *240, 247*
Millen, Senator Edward, *40*
Moffatt, Captain Hayward, *235, 238, 240, 250*
Monash, General Sir John, *104, 107, 143, 179, 205, 208*
Moran, Lord (Wilson, Charles M.), *78, 81, 86, 89, 91, 95*
Mortlock, Lieutenant Kenneth, *235, 250*
Morton, Ern, *151*
Muir, Corporal Cecil William, *121, 125*
Mullins, Private Arthur, *68, 125, 257*

N

Needs, Frank (aka John King), *98*

P

Pearce, Senator George, *40, 107*
Pettit, Corporal Leonard, *121*
Phillip, Governor Arthur, *164*
Porter, Lance Corporal Edward, *121*

R

Rawlinson, General Sir Henry, *226*
Robson, Private William, *68, 125*
Rostron, Private Allen, *227, 261*

S

Surname Index Kane, Private William, *208, 209*
Sampson, Lieutenant Reginald, *257*
Sassoon, Siegfried, *174*
Short, Corporal Jesse, *174*
Shout, Captain Alfred J., *63*
Slater, Corporal Henry, *247*
Somerset, Captain Charles Stabb, Alfred, *151*
Stacy, Lieutenant Colonel Bertie, *235, 240, 247, 252, 261*
Stanley, Peter, *68, 104, 118, 174*
Steen, Lieutenant George, *232, 235, 238, 240, 247, 250, 257*
Stevens, Private George, *208, 209*
Stokes, Private Ernest, *68, 209*
Sweeney, John J., *98*

Surname Index Walker, Lance Corporal Ernest, *125, 191, 209*

T

Taplin, Corporal Rollo, *5, 20, 23, 26, 34, 48, 58, 63, 68, 73, 115, 118, 121, 125, 130, 133, 185, 187, 195, 200, 203, 226, 227, 247, 257, 261*
Thompson, Alistair, *143, 144*
Tickner, Private Henry, *250, 252*
Traill, Lieutenant Sydney, *253*
Travers, Captain Ben, *18*
Turpin, Private John, *208, 209*

W

Wethered, Corporal George, *250*
Wilemett, Sergeant Earnest, *238, 247, 250*
Wintringham, Thomas,
Wolff, Captain Otto, *247*
Wood, Sergeant, *235, 238*
Woodford, Private Albert, *125*

Wren, John, *34*

Y

Youden, Major Herbert, *247*

Young, Sydney, *60*

www.ingramcontent.com/pod-product-compliance
Lightning Source LLC
Chambersburg PA
CBHW010717300426
44114CB00022B/2885